D0496287

Flexible Manufacturing

Related Titles from Butterworth–Heinemann

Applied Ergonomics Handbook
  Ian Galer

Computer Integrated Manufacturing: A total company
competitive strategy 2nd Edition
  Alan Weatherall

Handbook of Engineering Design
  Roy Cullum

Manufacturing Assembly Handbook
  Bruno Lotter

Manufacturing Cells: Control, Programming and Integration
  David Williams and Paul Rogers

Manufacturing Engineers Reference Book
  Dal Koshal

MRP II: An Integrated Approach
  Martyn Luscombe

Plant Engineers Reference Book
  Dennis Snow

Project Planning and Control 2nd Edition
  Albert Lester

Statistical Process Control 2nd Edition
  John Oakland

Successful Product Design
  Bill Hollins and Stuart Pugh

The Value of Advance Manufacturing Technology: How to assess
the worth of computers in industry
  Jerry Busby

*All books may be ordered from your local bookseller. In case of
difficulty please contact:*

Reed Book Services
PO Box 5
Rushden
Northants NN10 9YX
Tel: (0933) 58521
Fax: (0933) 50284

Flexible Manufacturing

David J. Parrish BSc MSc PhD MIMechE CEng

UNIVERSITY OF
LUTON
PARK SQ. LIBRARY

3402489273
621.78

Par.

4 DAY LOAN

BUTTERWORTH
HEINEMANN

Butterworth-Heinemann Ltd
Linacre House, Jordan Hill, Oxford OX2 8DP

PART OF REED INTERNATIONAL BOOKS

OXFORD   LONDON   BOSTON
MUNICH   NEW DELHI   SINGAPORE   SYDNEY
TOKYO   TORONTO   WELLINGTON

First published 1990
Paperback edition 1993

© Butterworth-Heinemann Ltd 1990

All rights reserved. No part of this publication may be reproduced in
any material form (including photocopying or storing in any medium by
electronic means and whether or not transiently or incidentally to some
other use of this publication) without the written permission of the
copyright holder except in accordance with the provisions of the
Copyright, Designs and Patents Act 1988 or under the terms of a licence
issued by the Copyright Licensing Agency Ltd, 90 Tottenham Court
Road, London, England WIP 9HE. Applications for the copyright
holder's written permission to reproduce any part of this publication
should be addressed to the publishers

British Library Cataloguing in Publication Data
Parrish, David J.
 Flexible manufacturing
 1. Flexible manufacturing systems. Manufacturing
industries
 I. Title
 658.514

ISBN 0 7506 1657 1

Library of Congress Cataloguing in Publication Data
Parrish, David J.
 Flexible manufacturing/David J. Parrish
 p. cm.
 Includes index
 ISBN 0 7506 1657 1
 1. Flexible manufacturing systems.   2. Computer integrated
manufacturing systems.   I. Title
 TS155.6.P38   1990   90-2181
 670.42'7–dc20   CIP

Photoset by BC Typesetting, Bristol BS15 5YS
Printed in Great Britain at the University Press, Cambridge

Preface

Purpose of this book
The aims of this book are to explain the following:

- flexible manufacturing systems (FMSs)
- The type of production technology where FMSs are applicable to a company
- how an FMS fits into a company's existing structure
- how an FMS can be successfully installed by a company
- how money can be made from the application of FMS

to company executives who need to know what FMS is all about, i.e. to managers, accountants, team leaders, project managers and directors. With a common understanding of the important basic elements of flexible manufacturing, constructive discussion between company executives of its potential applications is simplified.

Simplified approach
Computer integrated manufacturing (CIM) systems are playing an ever larger role in today's automation of industry. A specific area of CIM, flexible manufacturing systems, is a particularly complex application. FMSs are used for the control of metal-cutting machine tools in a mixed-batch-production system. The FMS is one of the most modern approaches to manufacturing a wide variety of products. FMSs are now being developed and installed in today's industry by suppliers and users of the technology.

Unfortunately, these technologically advanced systems have spread in manufacturing industry with an unnecessary amount of pain. This has been due to a lack of understanding of the concepts of FMS and to a shortage of skills required to install such systems.

This book is written to explain, on a non-technical level, the concepts of flexible manufacturing systems to company executives and engineers. It concentrates particularly on the manufacturing field of metal-cutting in the mixed-batch-production environment. It is concise and avoids the use of jargon to convey the principles of flexible manufacturing. It explains the

- technology
- applications
- advantages

of FMS for an executive to establish if the application of FMS is relevant to his or her company's needs. Diagrams are used wherever an illustration will convey a complex explanation better than a host of words.

FMSs are now a proven new technology

Flexible manufacturing systems provide an excellent training ground for companies wishing to introduce, or expand, their CIM facilities. An FMS includes, in one system, all the types of control hardware and software to be found in a factory which are otherwise integrated, in a piecemeal fashion, in other areas of CIM. It also provides a real added-value financial return once installed.

The implementation of flexible manufacturing will be a standard technology of the future just as CNC and CAD technology has emerged as a standard technology of today. FMS development has gone through a painful birth phase and is currently going through a slow growth phase. A non-painful growth is possible as present-day FMS technology is now based upon the integration of the established technology of computer-controlled machine tools. The specific area of mixed-batch-production for machining operations (metal-cutting) is highlighted in this book, although non-machining processes and assembly are just as applicable for flexible manufacturing technology.

A book for engineers and executives

Company engineers need to understand the terminology and technology of FMS to believe in and achieve the successful introduction of an FMS into a company. Company executives will be required to understand the benefits of the new technologies, in order to invest in the equipment and people with confidence, and to be sure of achieving positive financial returns for the investment. Many chief executives are aware of the pain involved in the installation of past systems. However, the technology has reached a stage where systems can now be installed with much greater ease, having been proven to work, due to the accumulation of hard-won experience from FMS suppliers and users alike.

Based on experience

This book is based on experience of installing FMSs, and endeavours to transfer the know-how to industrialists who believe FMS technology may be the right direction in which to go but who are not aware of the advances made in the field. Future systems will be increasingly installed, with the major functions in the system coming from a core of standard software. Installation times will be short. To achieve acceptance of FMS technology, the mystique and specialization that the executive always meets when such technology is discussed needs to be removed. This book aims to assist the understanding of what an FMS is – for the decision-takers of industry to gain a comprehension, and acceptance, of the new technology. The question, 'Why add a complex FMS host computer to my existing or new capital equipment (which already costs enough money)?' is answered. The answer is provided through the explanation of the FMS awareness, planning installation and application phases of a project.

Contents

Abbreviations

The following list includes the more common abbreviations that will be found in the world of computer integrated manufacturing, some of which occur in this book. As in all other specialist fields, the use of abbreviations is widespread; the meanings may thus differ from those used in other fields:

AC	area controller
AMT	advanced manufacturing technology
ASW	application software
ATFL	acceptance test function list
CAD(D)	computer-aided design (and draughting)
CAE	computer-aided engineering
CAM	computer-aided manufacture
CAP(P)	computer-aided planning (and processing)
CIM	computer integrated manufacturing
CMM	Coordinate measuring machine
CNC	computer numerical controller
CPA	critical path analysis
DA	data acquisition
DNC	distributed (or direct) numerical control
FAS	flexible assembly system
FDS	function design specification
FFS	fine function specification
FMC	flexible manufacturing cell
FMS	flexible manufacturing system
FOF	factory of the future
FTL	flexible transfer line
FW	firmware
HW	hardware
ISO/OSI	International Standards Organisation/ open systems integration
MDA	machine data acquisition
MIS	management information system
MRP	materials requirements (or resource) planning
MTL	multi-transfer line
NC	numerical controller
NPV	net present value
PC	personal computer
PLC	programmable logic controller
PO	production order
RC	robot controller
ROI	return on investment

SDA	system data acquisition
SFDC	shop-floor data collection
SP	sub-program
SR	subroutine
SW	software
TL	transfer line
WS	workstation

Chapter 1

Introduction to flexible manufacturing

The flexible manufacturing system (FMS) is the latest application of computer control to automate batch production manufacturing. It is the newest step in a long line of progressive innovations to raise the productivity of particular parts of industry.

1.1 The march of industrial progress

As the end of the twentieth century approaches, industry is beginning a new technical revolution the like of which has not been seen since the Industrial Revolution of the nineteenth century. Two hundred years ago a mass mobilization of the populace was carried out to provide the labour force for the emerging industries. These industries were revolutionized with the inventions of steam power and mechanized equipment. They provided a rise in productivity, compared to the previous cottage industries, which ensured the demise of the older methods. At the turn of this century, and continuing to the present day, the principles of scientific management have been developed to make the application of this work-force more effective.

In the past, cottage industries' flexibility to different market requirements was very high due to the labour-intensive methods used. However, such flexibility has not been required in the markets of the last two centuries. The markets accepted less product variety for the sake of cheaper mass-produced goods. This is now changing. The richer markets of today look for flexibility from their industrial suppliers to fulfil greater individual requirements. Purchasers want their own unique product – for example, customized cars and engines.

Industry can be broadly categorized into the service, process and manufacturing industries (Figure 1.1). Manufacturing industry has progressed through the phases of:

1. Industrialization
2. Mechanization
3. Automation (computerization)

and is now starting the phase of

4. Integration (linking)

1

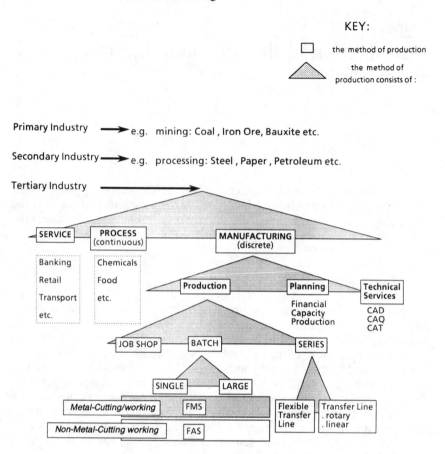

Figure 1.1 The area of application for FMS in industry

of the automated manufacturing processes. Mechanization of manufacturing processes has greatly reduced unit labour costs. Automation and integration of the information processes aim to further reduce the total manufacturing costs through more effective usage of production time and a greater availability of production data to enable effective planning of that available time.

From the middle of the twentieth century computers have increasingly been applied to manufacturing industry activities to replace 'non-productive' and costly labour. This has resulted in further increases in the levels of productivity. Computer applications occurred initially in the process industries and the technical and planning departments of manufacturing industry. The automation of manufacturing industry has been assisted by the introduction of digital computers in the 1950s and by integrated circuits (ICs) and microcomputers in the 1970s. The production activities of manufacturing have seen the advancement of computer applications, mainly in 'stand-alone' islands of automation: for example, CNC (computer numerical controller) machine tools and robots. The metal-cutting 'chip production' side of manufacturing is one of the latest and hardest areas to have been automated. The automation is now occurring on a large scale, and in certain ambitious companies production automation projects are also being integrated into the total factory environment.

Technology has advanced to the stage where these individual 'islands' can be integrated with each other. It is the integration of automation which is the new evolutionary phase dawning on manufacturing industry. The pressures of new, highly competitive, market environments, requiring flexibility and fast responses from industry, are forcing the introduction of this integration phase. Even traditional mass-production processes now strive for not only high volume but also flexible batch-oriented production. Even at the other extreme of manufacturing, job shops, which are highly flexible, manual-intensive, production systems, now require increased levels of productivity to be able to compete in a cost-conscious market (Figure 1.2).

The integration of automated industry is now recognized by the widely accepted label of 'computer integrated manufacturing' (CIM). Factory integration enables better organization of material and information flows. The main objective is to eliminate factory bottle-necks, thereby utilizing a factory's capacity better, be the bottle-necks a shortage of equipment, capacity or information. Part of the CIM concept is the application of FMS technology.

An FMS is a system in which all the aspects of CIM automation and integration are found in one, sometimes small, system. A machine tool is part of an FMS just as an FMS is a part of the total CIM environment. FMS is the 'sharp end' of CIM. It is where value is added to a product or piecepart, usually by cutting metal.

In the early 1980s FMS was a well-used buzz-word. It was described as the latest automation approach to cure the ills of manufacturing industry – an industry organized on contemporary technology which could not respond to the new markets requiring flexibility in production. Governments, the supply industries (computer- and machine-tool builders) and FMS users poured large amounts of money into FMS technology, and scores of projects were undertaken. The projects took longer to install than was originally foreseen. The industries (suppliers and end-users), discussed the situation from their own viewpoints and experience, leaving the impression to the potential FMS-user industries that FMS is a problem technology. This is not now the case as there have been many successes, despite the previous lack of knowledge and experience in the FMS-supplier and -user companies. The whole of the potential FMS-user industry can now embark on an FMS learning curve to use effectively the technology which has been developed and gain the benefits from it.

This book is intended to help just those companies who wish to advance along the learning curve.

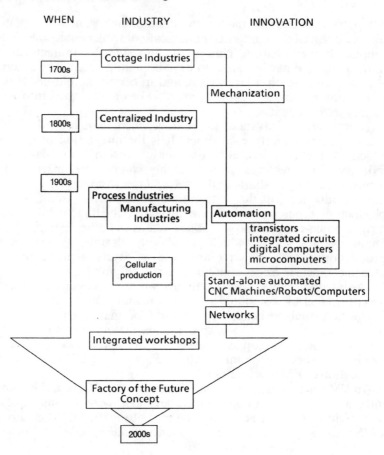

WHEN   INDUSTRY   INNOVATION

Figure 1.2 Innovations that have advanced the manufacturing industries

1.2 What is computer-integrated manufacturing (CIM)?

1.2.1 Industry

Industry is a generic description covering several activities which add value to a 'product' or provide a 'service'. The activities are carried out because it is believed there is a profitable market from the results of these activities. The three major categories of industry are primary (e.g. the winning of ore, minerals, etc., from the earth), secondary (e.g. the processing of ore and minerals into steel, for example) and the tertiary industries (e.g. creating goods such as cars). Industry is also categorized as service (e.g. transport, tourism), process (e.g. chemical production) and manufacturing (e.g. cars). The process industry is normally concerned with mass or batch production of end-products which have no

discernible breaks in their processing (and is therefore often called
'continuous production'). Manufacturing industry produces goods in
finite amounts (discrete production). The amounts can range from a
batch quantity of one (unit production) to that of hundreds of
thousands (mass production). The process industries have long been
automated and computerized. The manufacturing industries have been
automated to a certain degree but mainly in the mass-production
environments. The small-batch-production environments have been
automated since the late 1970s, with the introduction of CNC, but have
not had these islands of automation integrated into the total factory
environment (Figure 1.3).

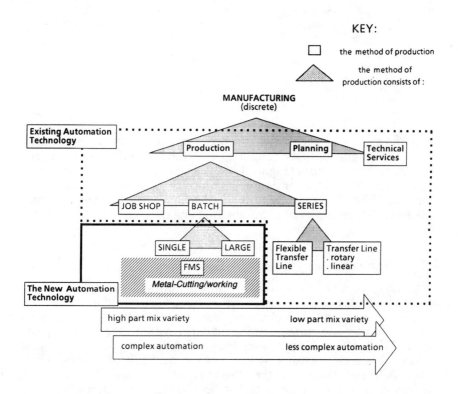

Figure 1.3 The current areas of flexible automation technology

1.2.2 Manufacturing

Manufacturing can be divided into direct production activities, where
value is added to a product as it is created, and the indirect functions,
such as planning. The purpose of the indirect activities is to support
the direct production activities. Manufacturing requires the various
activities as listed in Table 1.1. Each activity has a specific function to

Table 1.1 The major activities found in industry

Indirect	corporate planning
	design
	quality control
	production planning
	production control
	material requirements planning
	goods input
	testing
	storage
	dispatch
Direct	manufacturing
	machining
	welding
	grinding
	painting
	etc.
	assembly

fulfil and can be considered as a process with an input and an output. These inputs and outputs consist of material and information to and from the other activities (Figure 1.4). The activities are dependent upon each other for their information in order to be able to execute their functions. The total manufacturing system's effectiveness and efficiency will depend upon the levels of automation and the type of integration.

1.2.3 Integration

Until very recently integration of information and data transfer was always manual, usually using paper as the transfer medium. With the advent of computers, and electronic data communications, it has been possible to integrate manufacturing activities without the need to 'push' paper. Each of the functions in Figure 1.4 can be considered as an individual island in a total factory environment full of islands. These 'islands' 'stand alone' in the environment fulfilling their function regardless of whether their data has been transferred automatically or manually. They can individually perform their functions for as long as they have data to perform on. The integration of these activities through the automatic transferral of the data is the goal of CIM, which aims to automate and then integrate the direct and indirect activities of a factory.

The automation of the direct, and some indirect, production activities is classified under the heading of advanced manufacturing technology (AMT), which aims to automate and integrate all functions of a factory concerned with manufacturing operations such as design, production or quality, etc. A business concern also includes more organizational activities such as finance, marketing, etc. This is not the domain of AMT.

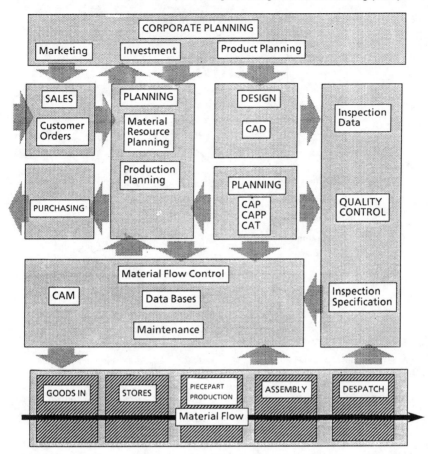

Figure 1.4 Data flow in the major manufacturing activities

AMT includes the automation of the manufacturing and engineering activities such as computer-aided manufacturing (CAM) and computer-aided engineering (CAE). Figure 1.5 helps to map this much abbreviated specialist area and put some of the terminology into context.

CAE includes:

1. CAD. Computer-aided design describes the use of a computer to support the construction of blueprints and schematic diagrams by an operator in order to design pieceparts, electrical layouts, etc. The operator uses the computer interactively by using:

   (a) Interactive plotting
   (b) Design draughting, or
   (c) Interactive design

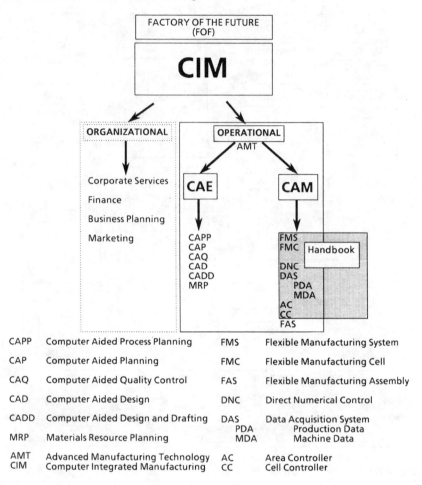

Figure 1.5 CIM technology

techniques. The results of the design process are displayed on a screen as a layout or a two- or three-dimensional colour picture. The output of a CAD system (e.g. numerical controller (NC) part programs) is used in other parts of the factory, i.e. a CAM CNC (computer numerical controller) production area.

2. CAQ. Computers are increasingly being used for the testing (computer-aided testing (CAT)) and quality assurance processes (computer-aided quality control (CAQ)). Measurement feedback is analysed to check if a single piecepart is within a specific quality tolerance. The accumulation of such feedback is also analysed to measure certain trends in the process in order to predict when a particular process is likely to go out of tolerance. Such statistical analyses allow pre-

emptive action to be taken to keep all pieceparts within tolerance. This task is also known as statistical process control (SPC).
3. CAP. Computer-aided planning is a generic term for the factory- or department-wide capacity planning functions. The function ensures that sufficient correct materials are provided to a facility for work to be performed at the facility. Also known as computer-aided process planning (CAPP), the function encompasses the construction of a manufacturing plan for a specific area's processes and production in terms of material (material requirements planning (MRP)), machines and equipment.

CAM includes:

1. Data acquisition systems (DAS), which include PDA (production data acquisition) and MDA (machine data acquisition). MDA is the automatic acquisition, and often the statistical analysis, of data from capital equipment. PDA is very much the same but includes the capture of other data such as those from operators (personnel data) or supply equipment.
2. DNC. Direct (or distributed) numerical control is the supply of NC programs to machine tools from a host computer and also their return-transmission to the host. This process eliminates the need for NC paper tapes and the subsequent tedious administration of the tapes.
3. FMS. A flexible manufacturing system is a group of capital equipment under an FMS host's control which organizes the supply of material, programs and tooling to the equipment to raise the equipment's productivity. A high degree of flexibility, in terms of simultaneous production of a mix of piecepart types, is possible when the host organizes the production.
4. FAS. A flexible assembly system has the same objectives as an FMS. However, the processes within the system are for the assembly of pieceparts rather than the machining of them.

1.2.4 Computers

The ubiquitous computer is an electronic machine (hardware) which executes a function according to a program (software or firmware). The following types of computer will be found within a CIM environment:

- mainframes
- minicomputers
- microcomputers
- personal computers (PCs)
- programmable logic controllers (PLCs)
- computer numerical controllers (CNCs)
- robotic controllers (RCs)
- workstations.

Standards for communications are being developed for these different types of computers. As the hardware comes from different manufacturers it is often a problem to get the hardware and software to talk to each other. Proposed and existing standards will enable different computers to talk to each other and exchange data. The communication types to be found are:

1. Transactions (a question and answer dialogue between two partner programs with alternate dynamic responses which are dependent upon the partner's action or reaction).
2. File transfer (neutral data exchange).

The manufacturing automation protocol (MAP) and the technical office protocol (TOP), based on the International Standards Organisation's open systems interface's (ISO/OSI) seven communication layers, are the best known initiatives in communication standardization. Thus a multi-computer system with a data exchange network can be created to provide the physical infrastructure upon which a CIM concept can be developed for a particular company's needs.

1.2.5 The CIM hierarchy

The activities in a factory's environment can be logically distributed into a hierarchy to run on a data exchange network system. There are five discernible levels of control or organization (Figure 1.6).

Within the CIM hierarchy, host systems are designed to control groups of machines and equipment or to organize facilities or data for the equipment. Levels 3 to 5 organize areas of a factory based on decisions taken from data received from other levels in the hierarchy. Control is the execution and monitoring of the decision by levels 1 and 2. These functional levels to be found in a factory environment are not to be confused with the much talked about seven ISO/OSI (International Standards Organisation/open system interface) layers upon which, for example, the MAP communication protocols are based. The CIM hierarchy levels support the organization of a factory to be able to carry out functions. The ISO/OSI levels enable communication between the functions to be found in a factory such as the data transfer between a CAD computer and an NC programming computer.

Levels 1 and 2 of the CIM hierarchy, consisting of CNC, NC, RC and PLC equipment, are where the control functions are executed. Levels 3, 4 and 5 define the organizational levels such as an FMS host, area controller or MRP computer, etc.

At the lowest level (1) of the hierarchy are the drives, motors, limit-switches, etc., of the production equipment. Level 2 includes the controllers which enable a machine to achieve an autonomous stand-alone capability. The CNCs, PLCs and microcomputers enable the machines to which they are dedicated to run unsupported from controllers on other (or on the same) levels of the hierarchy.

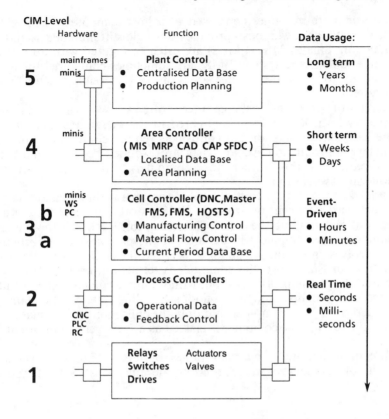

Figure 1.6 The CIM hierarchy

The dedication of controllers to equipment or functional areas results in decentralization of control in the hierarchy. This provides a greater total system reliability with a high system up-time. If any one part of the hierarchy fails the remainder may continue to function.

A production cell host computer can be installed (hierarchically) above the stand-alone machines to provide organization and monitoring of a group of such machines. This is level 3(a), where, usually, personal computers and minicomputers are installed. It is often dependent upon the size of the system (in terms of machines, transport, etc.) and complexity (in terms of software, functions, etc.), whether the manufacturing industries define these systems as:

1. Flexible manufacturing cells (FMC) – a small system, or
2. Flexible manufacturing systems (FMS) – large systems.

Some manufacturers of machine tools, particularly in West Germany, will call a single stand-alone machining centre a 'cell' which is flexible. To avoid confusion, FMS, wherever it is mentioned in this book, refers to two or more machines connected to a host computer. Each of the systems with an FMS host provides a single autonomous island of production. Small FMSs (FMCs) are often configured with up to four machine tools in the system. FMSs are sometimes configured for up to 40 machine tools but the average size is one of six to eight machine tools in a system.

Level 3(b), where the host computer is often known as a coordination or master host, is only ever configured in the hierarchy when two or more level 3(a) production cell controllers require coordination into an even larger production island. They are grouped together under the coordination of this master host computer to form the expanded autonomous workshop.

Level 4 configures the control level for an area within a factory (e.g. a production department or group of FMSs, stores, etc.). The input and output of material into the area is planned at this level, as is the capacity planning of the equipment in the area. If the planning for a particular area involves an interactive dialogue between the computer on this level and, say, an FMS host, the computer is termed an area controller. If not, and the planning is carried out without any feedback, the computer on this level is an open-loop shop-floor scheduling system. If no planning is carried out by the computer, but only the collection and evaluation of data from level 3, the computer is classed as a management information system.

The minicomputers and mainframes of level 5 provide the automation of the factory-wide or corporate functions. Such functions

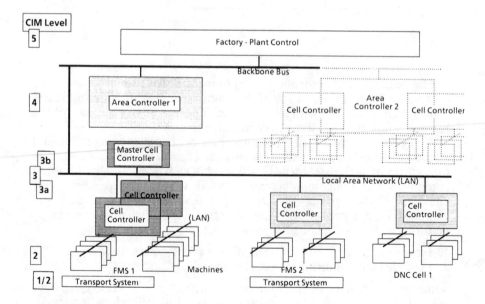

Figure 1.7 An example of a CIM implementation

include computer-aided planning (CAP), computer-aided design (CAD), material requirements planning (MRP), finance, marketing, etc. Figure 1.7 illustrates a potential implementation of cell and area systems based on this CIM hierarchy.

Each computer or controller, on each level, has its own functions to perform. To do this each controller needs specific data from its master on the next highest level. It also needs to return a specific amount of data to its master. A continuous filtered data transfer is required throughout the hierarchy. An interface specification is needed for each transition from level x to level $x+1$ (or $x-1$) to ensure successful networking of the integrated systems and stand-alone operation of the machines and production islands. At present the main instigators of full CIM technology application in Europe are the large automotive, aerospace or metal-working (i.e. cutting/fabrication) industries. It is rare for such total integration to be implemented by the much smaller companies, but it is now beginning to happen and can be done in a 'stepwise' fashion.

1.2.6 The application of CIM

A company makes money by adding value to a piece of material, i.e. in its new form a customer will buy the product at a price higher than the cost of adding the new value. Any increase in productivity to the value-adding processes is the most effective form of application for CIM. To date such increases have proved to be extremely difficult. Thus CIM integration has tended to be top-down rather than bottom-up. The automation and integration of the planning and design processes (CAPP, CAD) has largely succeeded, as seen by their widespread application, whereas industry has only seen the automation and not the integration of the metal-cutting manufacturing processes. FMS integrates the automated manufacturing processes on a cell basis. CIM techniques can integrate an FMS, and other processes, to each other and to the planning and design processes higher up in the hierarchy.

A bottom-up approach to integration, such as the implementation of an FMS, has the advantage that it starts with those processes which immediately increase the productivity of the added-value processes. Thus a company can be seen to earn money from an automation and integration project.

A final CIM solution for any company will be unique to that company and its specific requirements. The principles are, however, the same whatever the company. The practicable object of CIM is to produce:

- the right mix of pieceparts
- the right quantity of pieceparts
- at the correct time
- with the correct quality.

Successful application of CIM requires a structured approach. With such an approach the ideals of the factory of the future (FOF), whereby personnel and paper are all but eliminated from the factory as far as is possible, can be sought after. This futuristic aim of developing a FOF is evolutionary and not revolutionary. The most advanced and complex evolutionary phase of the FOF concept is FMS. An FMS is in itself a small factory. It can have all the functions, controls and organizational technologies, material and data flows, etc., integrated on a microcosmic cell level, that are also found as a macrocosm in a factory.

The lessons to be learned in installing an FMS are crucial to would-be factory-wide CIM users. FMS is not only one of the best training grounds for companies wishing to install CIM but also supplies an immediate return in terms of cost savings to those companies. FMS, remember, is the sharp end of CIM. FMS is the 'bottom-up' implementation of a system that provides added value to a piecepart or product. With proper systems integration it can work with the 'top-down' organizational processes such as MRP or CAD. As FMS is an event-driven material-flow system it can also be integrated into the world of just-in-time manufacture.

Chapter 2

What is FMS?

An FMS, when applied in a CIM environment, is a major investment. To see if FMS technology is relevant for a particular manufacturing enterprise it is necessary to describe exactly what an FMS is and what it can do for a company.

2.1 Evolution of FMS

FMS is the latest level of automation along an evolutionary road to achieve ever more productivity and flexibility from manufacturing equipment. At the start of this road machine tools were initially mechanized with manually driven axes using turn-wheels, screws and driveways, etc. Then the drive power became more sophisticated, using centralized pulley belts and, eventually, independent electrically powered drive motors. The control of these machines passed through the phases of manual, pneumatic or hydraulic logic control to electronic control. Computers, known as numerical controllers (NC), were dedicated to individual machines during the 1950s, or were even wheeled about amongst a group of machines, to control axis cutting speeds and positioning. The capability of NC computers has since been increased to control all peripheral equipment on the machine tools such as pallet-change tables, tool magazines and their contents, etc. These enhanced controllers, developed in the 1970s, became known as computer numerical controllers (CNC) and are still developing even greater capacities and capabilities.

In this way completely automatic self-contained machine units have developed. These are identified as 'stand-alone' CNC machines. However, the provision of data and materials to a CNC machine was, and mostly still is, completely manual. NC programs are loaded manually to the CNC using paper tape and tape punches/readers. Pallets are manually loaded on to the machines and then loaded with the fixtures and pieceparts. One of the first steps to lower the amount of manual intervention was the evolution of the down-loading of NC programs via a DNC link from an NC program storage computer. Loading of the machines with pieceparts was improved with the inclusion of a pallet-pool loading device for the different types of machine tools. This provided an 'in-machine buffer' for the machine to have perhaps a day's loading to work with. However, a great deal of manual preparation work was still required which interfered with the machine's main task of cutting metal (i.e. being productive). The next step was for a group of machines to be connected physically using a piecepart transport system. A cell concept eventually evolved where a host computer was able to take over many of the organizational tasks carried out by an operator which would have otherwise restricted the productivity of the machines. The major tasks of the host are to supply a group of machine tools with data, equipment and pieceparts, thereby decoupling the non-productive preparatory work from the productive manufacturing work. Operators, following host instructions, can prepare a machine with pieceparts and tooling whilst the machine tools are simultaneously working on other, previously prepared, pieceparts. Non-metal-cutting time is thus minimized. The computer is recognized as the 'FMS host'. Really modern FMSs also include a complete tool flow system as well as piecepart flows.

It was in the 1960s that D. T. N. Williamson of the British Molins company originally conceptualized and constructed such a logically and physically integrated machining system. Patents were taken out worldwide, of which the US patent is still valid. Initially the FMS control hierarchy was top-heavy with many functions centralized on the single FMS host computer. This computer was usually a mainframe due to the lower performance of the earlier available computers. The high cost of computers in those days also did not advance the cause of decentralizing the functions over several expensive computers. If the host malfunctioned then the whole FMS stopped. Today, with cheaper and higher-performance hardware and software, the FMS control hierarchy is much more decentralized. Many functions have been off-loaded from the host to the peripheral controllers in the FMS such as the CNCs and PLCs. This decentralization of the functions across more localized hardware results in a higher system reliability. If the host breaks down the FMS can still function, although not with such a high degree of automation and without integration. Alternative emergency strategies can be developed for the peripheral equipment to take over certain functions. For example, a transport system controller can take its instructions from an operator instead of the host computer. Figure 2.1 maps this evolution of automation up to the level of modern FMSs.

2.2 Definition of an FMS

An FMS is a collection of production equipment logically organized under a host computer and physically connected by a central transport system. The object of the FMS is to simultaneously manufacture a mix of piecepart types whilst being flexible enough to sequentially manufacture different piecepart type mixes without costly, time-consuming, change-over requirements between mixes. A particular piecepart mix can be manufactured simultaneously on one day and another mix on another day.

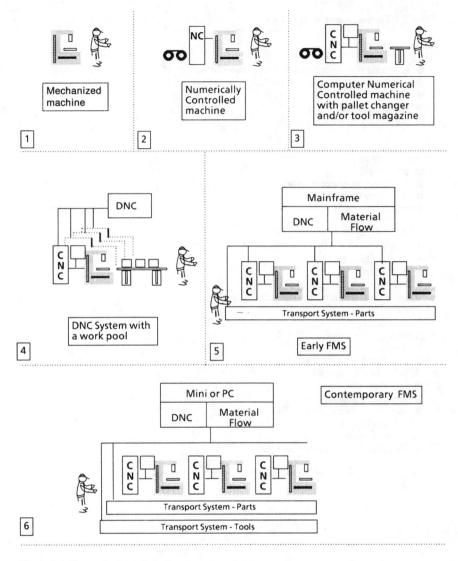

Figure 2.1 The evolution of FMS

2.2.1 FMS equipment

The capital plant in an FMS (Table 2.1) consists of two types of equipment – primary and secondary. The primary equipment adds value to the pieceparts being manufactured. Secondary equipment is used to support the primary equipment in achieving this goal. The primary equipment consists of work centres, which physically machine a piece-

Table 2.1 The equipment in an FMS

Primary equipment
Work centres
- universal machining centres (prismatic FMSs)
- turning centres (rotational FMSs)
- turning centres (rotational FMSs)
- grinding machines
- nibbling machines
  etc.

Process centres
- wash machines
- coordinate measuring machines
- robotic workstations
- manual workstations
  etc.

Secondary equipment
Support stations
- pallet/fixture load/unload stations
- tool commissioning/setting area
  etc.

Support equipment
- robots
- pallet/fixture/stillage stores
- pallet buffer stations
- tool stores
- raw-material stores
- transport system (AGVs, RGVs, robots)
  - tooling
  - pieceparts
- transport units (pallets/stillages)
  etc.

part, and process centres, which assemble, check or wash, etc., the pieceparts.

The conceptual layout of an FMS is illustrated in Figure 2.2 showing the modules which make up an FMS. All, or a subset, of the modules shown are required for an FMS user to be able to implement an FMS. For example, the tool flow module will not be required in every FMS. However, the FMS host module is, of course, always necessary. Table 2.2 illustrates the major functions required in an FMS to integrate the equipment into a working system. To successfully integrate the equip-

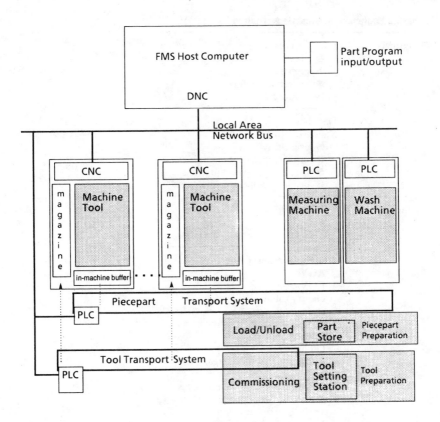

Figure 2.2 The conceptual layout of the modules in an FMS

ment into an FMS the know-how of three major FMS construction
parties are required:

● the FMS user
● the FMS host supply

and for automation control equipment supplier

● the machine tool builder and/or equipment supplier.

Table 2.2 Equipment and functions required for an FMS

Functions	FMS host computer ● plan ● prepare ● material/tool flow ● monitor
	Data base System control ● event-drive ● priority interrupts ● machine-coupled programs ● decoupled operator dialogues
Equipment	*Communication system* *Bus – LAN* *Star – Point-to-Point – Serial*
	Automatic material flow AGVs RGVs Gantry robots, etc.
	Automatic material flow Global store Local machine tool magazines

	CNC control of the machine tools
	● NC program process control
	● PLC peripheral control
	    pallet change-over
	    magazine control
	    pallet offset administration
	    tool offset administration
	    PLC/Micro/mini control
	    of process equipment
	    Coordinate measuring machines
	    Wash machines,
	    etc.

Universal machine tools
- Milling
- Drilling
- Turning
- Nibbling,
  etc.

Machine design for a mix production environment
- in-machine buffers
- tool magazine(s)
- NC program storage,
- etc.

2.2.2 Types of FMS

There are several methods to apply an FMS to a manufacturing environment. A sophisticated host can handle all the different methods so that the type of production executed in a manufacturing system can change during the lifetime of the FMS. The five types of FMS are:

● sequential FMS
  random FMS
  dedicated FMS
  engineered FMS
  modular FMS.

A sequential FMS manufactures one piecepart batch type and then planning and preparation is carried out for the next piecepart batch type to be manufactured. It operates like a small batch flexible transfer line. A random FMS manufactures any random mix of piecepart types at any one time. In contrast a dedicated FMS continually manufactures, for extended periods, the same but limited mix of piecepart batch types. Common for the very early FMSs is the engineered FMS type which manufactures the same mix of part types throughout its lifetime. It is a bespoke solution for an FMS user. A modular FMS, with a sophisticated FMS host, enables an FMS user to expand their FMS capabilities in a stepwise fashion into any of the previous four types of FMS.

2.2.3 Applications of FMS

The FMS philosophy has been applied chiefly in the following manufacturing areas:

  metal-cutting machining
  metal forming
  assembly.

Its concept has also been applied to:

  joining – welding (arc, spot), glueing
  surface treatment
  inspection
  testing.

By far the most widespread use of FMS technology has been in the metal-cutting areas of production.

2.2.4 FMS configurations

FMS layouts cover systems which include quantities of machines ranging from 1 to 60. Batch sizes can range from one-offs to a batch size in the thousands. Product variants may range from a type mix of only one to a mix of hundreds. A machine configuration of only one machine will not achieve the increased benefits of the larger systems but it is realistic to apply the FMS host abilities in cases where, for instance, a complicated tool organization is required.

2.3 The FMS host computer

The host computer can be configured from mini-, micro- or personal computer hardware with their corresponding operating systems and FMS software. The FMS software may consist of an FMS host supplier's standard FMS software plus any FMS user's system-specific application software required to 'tailor-make' the standard FMS software to a particular FMS's requirements (Figure 2.3).

The host often needs to have an interrupt handling capability and is usually a process computer. Minicomputers are suitable for FMSs or personal computers for smaller FMCs (cells). The host reacts to event-driven interrupts from the shop-floor equipment. This might be a

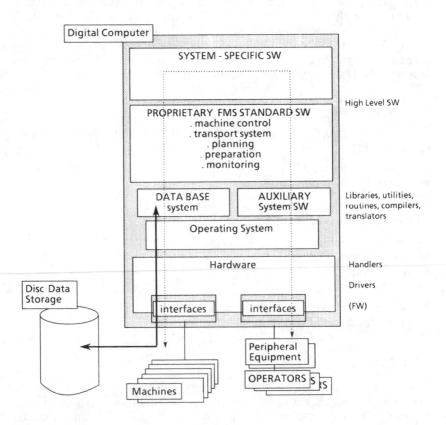

Figure 2.3 The system levels in an FMS host computer

machining centre reporting the end of an NC program run. The host
organizes the next event for the equipment (for example, the removal of a
piecepart from a machine). Such interrupts need to be administered in a
hierarchical priority. Alarm interrupts indicating a machine breakdown
are of a higher priority than a system message reporting a tool-life status
update. The type of FMS host hardware will really depend upon the size
of the FMS in relation to the consequences of applying a certain type of
hardware. An FMS with 50 machines producing, say, 60 percent of a
company's output will require a reliable computer with full data security
back-up (e.g. hot or cold standby hosts and/or data-shadowing techniques on back-up disc drives). Should such a host break down without
and standby back-up a company's production line could stop. For this
situation a process computer with these facilities is essential. In contrast,
a small company wishing to integrate just two machines may not find the
expense for such technical security justified. Thus a lower-cost personal
computer hardware solution would suffice. Often the hardware price, in
relation to the value of the machine tools having their automation levels
upgraded with a host computer, plays a major role to the FMS user. The
saying 'horses for courses' applies here.

2.4 FMS concepts

To understand the full potential that can be gained with the application of an FMS the concepts concerning FMS must be understood.
The concepts cover mixes, machine allocations, flows, planning and
scheduling.

2.4.1 System mixes

(a) Piecepart mix
The distinction must be made between:

● total piecepart mix
● planned piecepart mix
● 'live' order mix
● 'live' pieceparts.

The total piecepart mix is that mix which, over the months and years, the
FMS has the capability of manufacturing.
   The FMS host can organize the manufacture of a wide range of
various pieceparts within the given primary equipment's manufacturing
capabilities. The machines have a finite capacity for any particular
period in which production is to be planned. Several periods may be
planned of which only one mix of orders has been released and is therefore live, i.e. running in the FMS. Of this live order mix only a part of the
mix is actually in the system being manufactured at any one time, as the
FMS's capacity is usually less than that required to manufacture the

complete planned piecepart mix. A subset of the total live piecepart mix is manufactured simultaneously in the system. As pieceparts drop out of the system more pieceparts of the planned live mix can enter the system at the load/unload stations. These are the live pieceparts. Thus the FMS is constantly fed with new work.

(b) Piecepart mix types
Pieceparts can be physically classified as:

- prismatic (cuboid shape components – for drilling, milling, reaming, etc.),
- rotational (round cylindrical components) – for turning, grinding, etc.), or;
- hybrid (rotational and prismatic shaped components, e.g. a crank-shaft).

The benefits gained from applying group technology principles in an FMS's layout and machine selection during the design stage mean that FMSs are usually allocated to component mixes of either prismatic or rotational pieceparts. Hybrid systems are usually applied for prototype piecepart production but are not so common.

Rotational FMSs often differ in character from prismatic FMSs in that their batch sizes can be very large indeed. NC program times are shorter (often one or two minutes compared with an average of 20 min and sometimes 8 h for pieceparts in a prismatic FMS). Batches for rotational FMS may exceed 2000 in size. Thus many rotational FMSs take on the characteristics of flexible transfer lines which have the flexibility to rapidly change piecepart batch types. Pieceparts are delivered in stillages of sub-batch sizes of up to 50 pieceparts, whereas a prismatic FMS may well only have one piecepart on a pallet at one time. Rotational FMSs require only a fraction of the tool type quantities to be found in a prismatic FMS. The tooling is also, of course, different.

(c) Machine allocation mix
An operation on a piecepart requires an NC program loaded into a machine tool's controller for the machine to execute the operation. An FMS operation can be considered, then, as a single NC part program. The NC part program will itself consist of several operations, each one better known as a cutting operation.

The allocation of the work centres to machine the different operations of a piecepart is defined as either:

- interchangeable allocation, or
- complementary allocation.

If a group of machines are truly interchangeable they are identical physically and are identically equipped with tooling, NC programs, pallets, etc. Subsequently that specific piecepart's FMS operations can be executed at one or other of the several alternative machines (Figure 2.4).

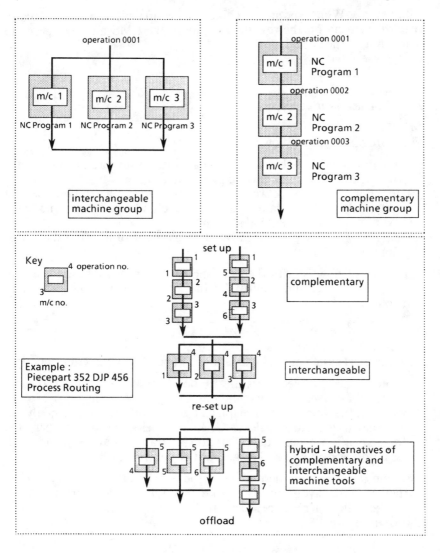

Figure 2.4 Process routings in an FMS

If the machines are complementary they are so equipped that a piece-part's first operation is to be carried out at one machine (or interchangeable group) and the next operation is to be carried out at another machine (or group). A single complementary machine will be a bottleneck machine if it has a very low capacity or there is no interchangeable machine to replace it when it breaks down. A machine need not be mutually exclusive to any interchangeable groups of machines. Such machine allocations are laid down in the host's process routing master data records. Which specific machine in a group a piecepart will actually visit will depend on the real-time events in the FMS and the real-time scheduling of the host.

2.4.2 Further basic concepts

(a) System flows
There are three types of flow in an FMS:

(a) material flow (physical)	– between the machines, transport system, buffer stores and processing station
(b) tool flow (physical)	– between the tool store, assembly, setting stations and the machine tool's magazine load/unload station
(c) data flow (logical)	– between the different control levels in the FMS.

Each type of flow is critical to the success of production and requires careful monitoring and control by the FMS host and the peripheral controllers.

(b) Transport system types
The transport system in an FMS layout can be of two types in principle:

1. Random access (pieceparts are randomly pulled out of a transport system for delivery to a machine, e.g. a loop conveyor).
2. Addressable (pieceparts are picked up at one station, e.g. by an automated guided vehicle (AGV), and delivered to another; the transportation from source station to target station is under a transport system's control, e.g. an AGV controller).

The choice of system design from these characteristics results in a particular FMS layout and is dependent upon the piecepart mix to be produced. The difference between an FMS's layout and configuration is shown in Figure 2.5.

(c) Parameterizable system
The most important functions of an FMS host are illustrated in Figure 2.6. A sophisticated FMS host will enable the FMS host supplier or FMS user to parameterize the host to the FMS's particular configuration.

Many functions of an FMS host are common to all system layouts. It is possible to parameterize the functions to the physical layout of a particular FMS. For example, the interface to two or four machines should not make a diffference to the control algorithm in the host. Some functions will, however, be unique to a layout and have to be developed uniquely for that system.

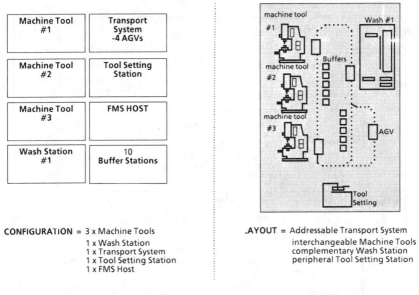

Figure 2.5 The concept of an FMS configuration and layout

(d) Host organizational control

An FMS host should be designed around the following major concepts:

The principle for a host in controlling an FMS should be that of organization. The host computer plans work for an FMS, instructs the operators in the tasks to be carried out, organizes the transport of the pieceparts and tooling and monitors the FMS for progress and errors. The host is an event-driven organizer awaiting the occurrence of events and reacting to them according to a plan. It does not initiate or maintain control of the equipment. This is carried out by the local CNC or PLC equipment. The host organizes an event and passes on permission for the local controller to start a process.

Decoupled planning. Planning of work for the FMS is carried out with an operator using the host computer interactively. The planning should be isolated from the real-time control of the FMS software. The host should not schedule work directly to the machines but should support the operator in calculating the capacity of the system for a given work-load. In this way the pieceparts will not be committed to a specific machine, of a group of interchangeable machines, until the last possible moment. Thus, should a machine in the group break down, the piecepart is still free to go to another alternative interchangeable machine. In this way it is possible to maintain the flexibility of the FMS's material flow.

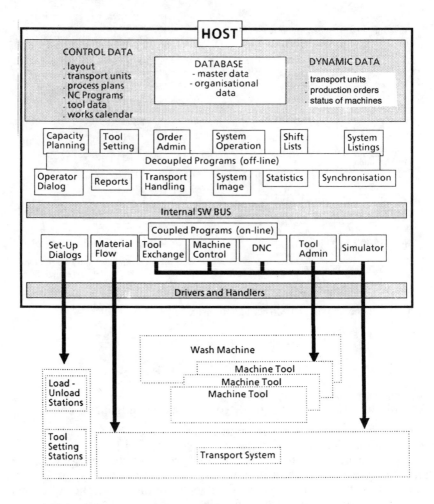

Figure 2.6 The major FMS host functions

Direct real-time schedule control. Planned work is only allocated to a specific machine when the individual piecepart has been set up in a fixture on a pallet and a machine is available, with all its necessary equipment and programs, to process it. The object of the host is to keep the expensive capital equipment utilized by supplying it with work. This is best achieved when preparatory work is carried out simultaneously whilst the machine is still working. The host organizes the preparation and transportation of the work so that it is already available to the machine when it next requests some work. The best machine utilization can be obtained when a machine's layout includes an internal machine buffer. The host can then organize this internal buffer to be always loaded with work. If this buffer is always loaded with work there will always be work available for the machine to transfer immediately into the spindle's work area. Pieceparts are moved from a machine under the organization of the host to other machines, or to a system buffer station, if the next machine in a piecepart's process route is busy and cannot accept a piecepart into its buffer.

2.4.3 FMS host–operator interfaces

The host manages the interfaces between the operators and the FMS. These host-driven dialogues should be based on a menu and mask system for ease of use. The operator can use screens, terminals and printers for these functions.

In order to prepare a piecepart for manufacture it must be set up on a transport unit, such as a pallet, containing a fixture. The tools must be set and loaded into the machines' magazines. These operations are carried out by operators receiving instructions from the host. They acknowledge them to the computer when they have completed the tasks.

Menu-mask dialogues. The operator can instruct the host to carry out tasks using a selection of menu and dialogue sequences at a screen terminal. Common tasks are the administration of master data or the planning of work. The menus should be hierarchically accessed and initiated using pre-allocated function keys. An example of functions that should be obtainable using mask dialogues are:

  main menu
  system mimic picture
  production planning
  NC program administration
  tool administration
  transport unit administration
  system servicing
  master data administration
  works calendar
  report-log system
  management reports.

The menus should enable access to the masks for the operator to both input and output the required data. Such masks are often protected by passwords so that only authorized access to the system is possible.

Printer output. Alarms and system messages from subordinate controllers should be typed out on a printer automatically. Alternatively these messages should be logged for dumping on a printer at a later date. The message-logging system should be parameterizable. A separate logging printer is preferable, where all alarms are printed with a time and date for the provision of an immediate hard copy.

2.4.4 Decentralized hardware/software system design

Standardization of FMS hardware, where possible, and the decentralization of software functions, provide the advantages of higher system maintainability and up-time for an FMS user. If the host breaks down the FMS can continue to produce, although with a degraded productivity level. The local controllers can take over many functions originally carried out by the host.

Replicated software in the controllers of the same level, for the same functions, simplifies updating or debugging of the software. When the same hardware is used, where possible in the FMS a simplified replacement strategy for inoperative hardware is possible.

Chapter 3

Why use an FMS?

Suppliers to the market of equipment containing machined pieceparts are finding that their customers require increased flexibility from them whilst they will not accept higher costs for this requirement. The machining systems of today must provide not only flexibility but also high productivity to provide low-cost goods.

3.1 Modern market requirements

The now established trend of higher customer demands on suppliers is not a new one but it is becoming increasingly more imperative and encompassing. Originally the consequences affected mainly the production area of assembly. Assembly of mass-produced parts into various end-products achieved product variety (e.g. different coloured cars of the same standard type). However, the demands are now reaching into the manufacture of the very pieceparts which make up the end-product.

For many traditional single-design products the days of mass production to achieve low-cost manufacture for these mass markets are gone. The new wealthy customers, who no longer need to concern themselves with purchasing only the essentials of life, can insist on individual models of the non-essential goods. The greater numbers of competing producers for product types means that the manufacturers must cater for these customers' tastes to sell their products. Increased competition since the late 1960s has changed the manufacturing environment for end-user products which were traditionally in the mass-production market (e.g. automobiles). Recently the increase in competition has also had the same effect on the piecepart components of such products (e.g. automobile engines and their component parts). Cars no longer need to just look different. They must actually be different. Engines of today are old-fashioned within a few years. Engine pieceparts are improved or new processes or materials are found continuously.

The result of such a competitive market is that the products' and their pieceparts' life cycle are decreasing. Customers put ever increasing demands on their suppliers. These demands are summarized in Table 3.1. Production equipment must be able to keep pace with these changing requirements.

Table 3.1 Customers' demands on suppliers

The highest quality and precision
High product variety
Frequent product design changes
Variable batch sizes
Short delivery times
Competitive prices
Fast reaction to market changes

To accommodate these requirements from the customers, product suppliers are being forced to change their type of production from mass-production to batch-production manufacture, not only in assembly but in the more complex area of machining. Production facilities must not only produce smaller batches of pieceparts but also an increasingly large mix of different batches – simultaneously and economically.

The old traditional methods of production involved the installation of a one-off manufacturing facility, a transfer line (TL), which was dedicated to the mass production of only one, or (if high change-over effort was acceptable) very few piecepart varieties. These systems are very productive, in terms of unit costs of production for each part manufactured, but they are very inflexible. Alternatively, where batches of differing part types are needed, a jobbing-shop environment is necessary. This is often a manually organized method of production, to maintain the high levels of flexibility required. Increased levels of productivity were often obtained with the application of group technology principles. However, although manually organized jobbing shops are highly flexible, the achievement of the levels of productivity found in TLs will never be possible due to the amount of machine change-over effort required.

These extremes in production methods are becoming less frequently technically applicable or economically justifiable. No customer will buy the expensive goods from such systems when they are purchaseable from one of the many alternative competitor suppliers who have found an alternative means of production to meet the buyers' demands.

The alternative means is the application of FMS technology where high levels of automation enable flexibility and productivity. This emerging method of manufacturing aims to solve the two following problems, which have conflicting objectives:

● high-capacity utilization and throughput
   with
   low work-in-progress

● high productivity
   with
   high flexibility

The use of a host computer integrates individual automated machining systems into an FMS to achieve these objectives. Such an FMS is also integratable into the total production environment, through the principles of computer-integrated manufacturing, to maximize the benefits obtained within the FMS by dovetailing the FMS into the total factory.

3.2 Modern manufacturing methods

FMS technology, as an alternative means of production, has been evolving since the mid-1960s. This application of computer technology to manufacturing enables a producer to tailor its factory facilities to meet the demands of its customer. FMS users require a system which is expandable, in terms of hardware and software functions, as and when they can afford them. They also need a system which can be integrated into their whole production environment. Present-day computer technology provides affordable systems which can be connected to all the other manufacturing activities in a factory through CIM data networks.

The industries which originally drove the investment in FMS applications were:

- automotive (heavy and light)
- automobile pieceparts
- aerospace
- machine-tool builders.

These are highly competitive industries where the product variance, with small to medium batch sizes, and the customers' demands, necessitate high quality and competitive prices. Through the know-how obtained from these large investments, FMS suppliers are now providing smaller low-cost solutions which are more applicable to smaller companies.

3.2.1 Advanced manufacturing technology (AMT) to increase productivity

The major objective of automation is to maximize and then utilize the available capacity of a machining centre. However, the available capacity for a machine to carry out productive work is never 100 percent. Losses in the theoretical availability of a machine tool due to various technical or organizational reasons are listed in Table 3.2.

A machine tool only earns money (i.e. adds value to the piecepart) when it is cutting metal. When it is idle it is costing money. A machine, or system of machines, has a given capacity level to which the machine utilization can be increased and maximized. Through the automation of the causes of machine down-time one can reduce the loss in machine availability and therefore increase machine utilization. This can be achieved through:

1. Automation of the cutting process:
    (a) CNC applications
    (b) adaptive control
    (c) multi-spindle operations
    (d) multi-axis operations

Table 3.2 Losses in machine availability

Technical reasons
- cutting conditions
- setting-up and resetting (tools/pallets/fixtures)
- performance gaps
- adjustments and positioning
- tool exchanging (load/unload)
- piecepart exchange (load/unload)
- piecepart set-up

Organizational time losses
- rescheduling
- shut-downs
- shift usage
- underloading capacity

2. Automation of the preparation processes:
   (a) load/unload, adjustment, settings, etc., of the piecepart to/from the machine
   (b) tool exchanges
   (c) piecepart exchanges within the machine.

The organizational losses can also be reduced through greater utilization of the production facilities:

   (a) flexible production equipment
   (b) automation of the production control processes
   (c) integration of the production equipment handling:
       (i) NC programs
       (ii) pieceparts
       (iii) pieceparts
   (d) integration of stores, process and transport functions

via system data collection and processing.

For the time a piecepart is in a job shop, 95 percent can be for moving it around and storing it. Only 5 percent of the piecepart's time is on a machine. Of this 5 percent up to only 30 percent of its time is actually productive cutting time. For the other 70 percent of its time the piecepart is being set up, gauged, positioned or just waiting on the machine. This must be considered in relation to the availability of a machine tool upon which it is intended to cut the piecepart.

The maximum measured availability of a machine tool to cut metal and add value to the piecepart is often in the range of 30–40 percent of total available time. This will depend upon a machine's design characteristics and the production mix it is working on. Unavoidable production losses (spindle positioning, NC tool changes) can account for 20 percent of non-cutting time. Technical disturbances amount to 10 percent and organizational disturbances may total 15 percent (waiting for operators, pieceparts, etc.). Setting and testing the machine can account for another 15 percent losses, while piecepart measuring, etc., can lose a further 10 percent of the time available for production.

Through increasing the levels of automation (NC, DNC, FMS), AMT philosophy aims to increase a machine's productivity. A machine's percentage 'loaded for work' time can be increased with the following orders of magnitude:

Level of automation	% time work in m/c
Level 1 – a stand-alone machine (NC)	5 percent
Level 2 – a stand-alone machine with CNC tool exchange	26 percent
Level 3 – a stand-alone machine with CNC tool and piecepart exchange	39 percent
Level 4 – a machine connected to a DNC host for NC program	45 percent
Level 5 – a machine integrated into an FMS exchange	85 percent

If a machine in an FMS has work on it for 85 percent of its time, and the host organizes that the supply of work to that machine is continuous, the utilization of that machine (spindle cutting metal) can, amazingly, approach 70 percent or even more.

(a) CNC stand-alone machines
Numerical controllers (NC) are now commonly installed for simple automation tasks. Each NC is dedicated to a single machine. This is one of the lowest levels of automation possible. Only the axes of the machine come under the control of an NC computer which refers to a part-program to automate the machining process. This is the simplest level of a stand-alone machine. Setting up the machine for new piecepart types is entirely manual.

The next level of automation is that when, for instance, the tool-exchanging facilities, i.e. the tool magazine contents and load/unload dialogues, are automated under the NC's supervision. The NC configuration to achieve this is often expanded with the addition of an integrated programmable logic controller (PLC) to cater for the extra functions. This enhanced control configuration is commonly known as computer numerical control (CNC), where equipment, peripheral to the machine tool, comes under the CNC's organization.

The third level of stand-alone capability is achieved by increasing the level of automation, with a further PLC if necessary, to include the piecepart load/unload functions. The setting of the piecepart, on to pallets which are already positioned on the machine, is still manual at this stage. When the machine has the ability to process several part types randomly (with a larger mix of tools in the magazine and the capability to accommodate several piecepart types in the machine) the machine takes on a characteristic of universality. These machines are known as universal machining centres and are the machine types that can be most successfully integrated into an FMS.

(b) Direct numerical control (DNC)
A further aid to automation is to install an NC program storage computer which can transfer the relevant program to the relevant machine controller on operator request. This eliminates the non-productive tasks of manually loading a program by paper tape and the subsequent administration of the tapes. Such a system is known as a distributed or direct NC system (DNC). It is the first step in integrating the CNC machine into a CIM environment. Modern DNC systems also include a great deal of data collection and even statistical analyses of the data for management reports.

With each increasing level of automation the machine's waiting time is reduced as the changeover and resetting tasks are executed automatically and simultaneous to production. This is possible provided the operator has carried out the preparatory work. The machine can continue cutting the piecepart whilst the operator prepares the work and tools up for the next job. FMS is the highest level of flexible automation for a group of machines based on this principle.

(c) Flexible manufacturing systems (FMS)
As indicated in the preceding section, real increases in productivity occur when several stand-alone machines are brought together into a cell under the organizational control of a cell host computer. An FMS can be considered as a group of CNC or DNC work centres which are connected physically with a transport system and logically under the organization of the manufacturing host computer.

The aims of FMS are listed in Table 3.3.

3.2.2 Types of FMS

There are several ways to apply an FMS to the manufacture of a part-mix. These are highlighted in Table 3.4.

3.2.3 The object to be achieved by an FMS

A study, carried out with West German manufacturers, has shown the major aims of installing an FMS to be:

- decreased lead times   *high priority*
- increased throughput
- increased machine utilization
- improved due-date reliability
- decreased store-inventory levels
- decreased work-in-progress
- increased quality   *low priority*

Table 3.3 The aims of FMS

To reduce costs
- better utilization of the production equipment
- reduction of stocks (e.g. work in progress – capital)
- shorter throughput times
- reduction of piecepart unit costs

To increase technical performance
- increased production levels
- greater product mix
- simultaneous product mix manufacture
- integration of the production system into the factory's logistical system
- smaller batch sizes (one-offs possible)
- shorter or zero change-over or re-set-up times

To improve order development
- shorter lead times/delivery times
- determination of production capacities

To assist future corporate security
- increased competitiveness
- increased quality
- improved company image

Table 3.4 Types of FMS

Part-mix oriented	
Dedicated	A long-term, fixed, known part-mix
Random	Unknown future part-mix
Engineered	System developed for only one part-mix
Flexibility oriented	
Potential	Part routings are fixed (scheduled) until a machine breaks down – replanning required
Actual	Part routings are not fixed until a machine calls for work (event-driven) – no replanning needed at machine breakdown

3.3 Types of flexibility

FMS technology is a process to simultaneously manufacture different parts in the shortest time possible, with the highest quality and at the lowest costs possible. To do this a maximum of management information must be available for the FMS host to work with. When this is achieved there are several types of flexibilities available to an FMS user. These are summarized in Table 3.5.

The flexibilities found in FMSs supplied to FMS users concern two areas of interest:

1. FMS user flexibility
2. FMS supplier flexibility.

Table 3.5 Types of FMS flexibility

Type	Description	Characteristic	Use
FMS user	Instant (i) (ii)	Flexible allocation of machines	Handling of disturbances Real-time scheduling
	Immediate (i) (ii) (iii)	User operation (flexible use of FMS by operator)	Bottle-neck planning DNC mode Urgent orders
	Short term	Tactical allocation of FMS to work	Different part-mix
	Long term	Strategic allocation of FMS to work	Different mixes of part-mixes
	Implementation flexibility	Machine tool flexibility Product flexibility Operational flexibility	Universal machines NC administration Process planning
FMS supplier	Hardware	Expandable configurations	Tailor-made configuration
	Parameterizable data base	Independence from FMS supplier for creation of the data base	Tailor-made data base
	Parameterizable functions	Independence from FMS supplier for application of functions using the data base	Tailor-made functions

Figure 3.1 illustrates how these different types of flexibilities can be used by an FMS user.

FMS user flexibility. The first area is that in which the FMS user is interested. This is the most important area. The available flexibilities are provided for the FMS user to be able to satisfy the demands of their customers.

FMS supplier flexibility. The second type of flexibility concerns the method of applying FMSs. This is of extreme interest to the FMS host supplier. Every FMS application is different, and no FMS supplier can start from scratch to supply a new FMS host solution every time for each new FMS user. A supplier's solution needs to be flexible enough to integrate different machine types into different FMS configurations and layouts for different product mixes. This also interests the FMS user as supplier costs can be minimized if the functions have been standardized over as many different systems as possible.

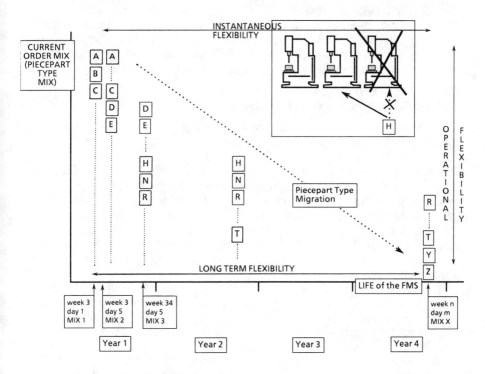

Figure 3.1 The different types of flexibility

When these two types of flexibility can be achieved an FMS solution, to the satisfaction of both FMS supplier and user, is possible. The present FMS developments have shown that these two aims are not contradictory.

3.3.1 FMS user flexibility

There are five types of FMS user flexibility. Each one brings a particular advantage to the user of the FMS. They are:

1. Instantaneous flexibility
2. Operational flexibility
3. Short-term production flexibility
4. Long-term flexibility
5. Implementation flexibility.

The first three flexibilities can be obtained with the FMS host using the same data base. With the fourth type the data base needs to be modified (updated) or completely changed. All five types of flexibility should be achievable on the same hardware and software.

(a) Instantaneous flexibility
There are two types of instantaneous flexibility which require the ability
of the host to provide flexible machine allocation. When alternative
routings for pieceparts, through an FMS, are available, a high level of
flexibility can be achieved to avoid system disturbances such as:

- machine breakdowns
- queuing of pieceparts on to machines.

Both disturbances would otherwise end up with the system stopping as
bottle-necks are created in the material flow.

Alternative routings for the handling of machine breakdowns. An FMS
may consist of several machining centres. The most flexible type of
FMS is that where all the piecepart types, for all their operations, in all
pallet/fixture set-ups, can visit any of the available universal machining
centres to be processed. This is possible when all the machining centres
are interchangeable for all the machining operations. Each machine
needs to be prepared with the same tool mixes and NC programs for each
operation to be interchangeable.
   If one of these machine-tools breaks down the production of pieceparts is not prevented as the pieceparts can continue visiting the other
remaining interchangeable machine tools in the system. This would not
be the case if there were a single bottle-neck machine in the system with
no alternative machine to take over from it.
   A transfer line does not have this flexibility. The machines may be
configured in such a system radially (rotary transfer) or linearly (transfer
line). If any of the machines breaks down, and it is a bottle-neck
machine, it will stop production on the whole line. This can only be
avoided when any of the machines are duplicated, as in a multi-line
transfer. Most machines have provision for an internal buffer storage.
On average only two or three pallets, with work on them, cannot be
processed further when an interchangeable machine breaks down as it is
only these few pallets which are stuck in the machine's buffer. All other
loaded pallets are free to visit the remaining working machines as they
are not dedicated to any machine. The system remains instantaneously
flexible to technical disturbances as no fixed schedule has taken place at
the planning stage. This type of flexibility is provided as a support to
production throughput. Machine disturbances are not a desired system
characteristic but they are unavoidable.

Alternative routings for a simultaneous live piecepart mix. A highly
desirable characteristic is this next level of flexibility. Organizational
machine-utilization losses are minimized when a mix of piecepart types
are manufactured live in the FMS at the same time. The operators load
pallets/fixtures with work so that as soon as a machine has the capacity
for further work one of the previously prepared piecepart types is ready
to be transferred into the machine. When work is always ready for any of
the machines in the system none of the machines needs to be short of

work. The restrictions on the live mix size are the quantities of pallets/fixtures, tool sets in the magazines and the system capacity. The actual routing through the system is never determined for each piecepart until the last minute (i.e. real-time scheduling). There is not only a mix of routings for each piecepart, of which one is chosen in real time, but also a mix of pieceparts, with their relevant routings, to be chosen for transportation to a machine. Not all FMS host solutions provide this level of flexibility. A machine tool which does not have an internal buffer will not block any pallets from visiting other machines if that particular machine breaks down. However, in the normal running mode such a machine has to wait on the transport system to take finished work away and resupply it with fresh work. For systems whose NC programs last, say, 2 hours, this may not be a problem.

(b) Operational flexibility
Immediate user operation flexibility is required for the operator to be able to use their FMS in their manufacturing environment as they desire. Thus operators can plan their production and run it automatically or intervene and make immediate operational changes as they see necessary.

Planning. During the planning operation the operator requires the flexibility to make adjustments for any production bottle-necks that may ocur due to the current mix of piecepart types planned. The operator may wish to modify a piecepart's process route temporarily or reduce the batch quantity size.

Rush orders. Often the need to immediately allow a production order into the system without any planning is required. These urgent orders will affect the due dates of the orders already planned as the rush order(s) will take priority and use up the machine capacity originally reserved for the planned order mix. The insertion of 'dummy' orders may offset the disruption to planned due dates caused by rush orders.

Machine mode switching. Often the mode that the machine tools work in requires switching (from automatic to DNC and back). This would be suitable for maintenance operations or as another means to push rush orders through the FMS by putting a machine under manual control. In DNC mode the machines can be used without reference to any planning or host-generated transport orders. This mode can be used to test new NC part programs.

(c) Short-term production flexibility (mix of current job mixes)
A short-term flexibility provides the tactical manufacturing capability to process a mix of production order mixes. The host computer data base should be large enough for the host to provide a type of flexibility that is advantageous over a short-term horizon. A mix of piecepart types may run live in the FMS at one time for a particular period (say several hours or one shift). However, as the work is completed, during the day or week,

more work is loaded into the FMS to keep the capital equipment utilized. This new work, loaded into the system, need not constitute a mix of the same piecepart types (as would be the case in a dedicated FMS).

New piecepart types can be added into the dwindling live mix. Thus the current live mix is constantly changing. The mix at the beginning of the week may be completely different from that which will run on the FMS at the end of the week. This short-term flexibility ensures that the FMS (under the host's organization) is not dedicated to a particular mix of piecepart types but is random in nature. This brings many advantages to the FMS user who can work in a true jobbing-shop batch production environment but still remain highly productive due to the integration of high automation levels. A single batch of one piecepart can be loaded into the FMS or several new batches of varying batch sizes.

The greater the number of different piecepart types that can be manufactured simultaneously the higher is the machine utilization (as there is always work prepared for any of the machines to work process). In this way the manufacturer can respond quickly to changes or differences in the market and its demands or to a changing mix of customers and their required product types.

(d) Long-term production flexibility (mix of future job types)
A strategic flexibility is needed over the life of the FMS. The FMS user has a manufacturing strategy to produce his pieceparts (e.g. number of pallet set-ups or operations per piecepart type). This strategy, as well as the piecepart mix, is likely to change over a long period.

The life cycle of an FMS is probably 10 to 15 years. By this time the machine tools themselves are likely to require physical replacement. Economically the capital equipment may be written off in 5 to 7 years. Either way, during the lifetime of an FMS the product mix requiring manufacture on the FMS at the start of its life will be completely different, in type and form, from that found on the system at the end of its life cycle.

An FMS host should be able to have its data base modified and updated to cater for new product types, process routings, tool type updates, etc. In this way, over the years of using the FMS, it should be flexible enough, without program code changes, to adapt to the new product mixes that will occur. This type of flexibility is known as 'production flexibility'.

(e) Implementation flexibility
There are various flexibilities required in an FMS for which the host should have the capability of handling but which are not functions of the host. For example, the CNCs which are installed into an FMS must have the flexibilities to manage tools and Pert programs, etc. These flexibilities, or lack of them, should not require host software changes for whichever configuration and layout of system the host is implemented. If the host's software requires changing it usually indicates that the

equipment controllers do not have sufficient intelligence to be fully integrated into an FMS. The end result would be a degraded level of integration, automation and therefore flexibility.

1. Equipment flexibility
The equipment included in an FMS must have the capability for full integration into the FMS. The machine tools and transport system are good examples where non-complete integration will decrease the flexibility that can be available in a system.

Machine tool. For full FMS flexibility the CNC of a machine must be fully integratable into the system. Decreased levels of CNC ability will result in degenerated levels of FMS ability. Assuming the machine's CNC has full logical ability to integrate with an FMS host, the most suitable type of machine tool to physically integrate into an FMS is a universal machining centre. These machines have automated pallet exchange, spindle positioning, DNC, tool management, etc. Such a machine is then physically capable of machining different part types in a random sequence to achieve the benefits of FMS.

Transport system. The transport system may well need the physical flexibility to carry different transport units (pallet types, stillages, trays, plattens, etc.) along the different routings in an FMS. If the transport controller cannot organize the transportation in an FMS, then the host will have to do it. If the host breaks down there will be no transportation as this function is not a decentralized function.

Product flexibility. The CNC of a machine tool can run different part-programs. These programs may be an update or a modification of a program for the same part type. Through the FMS host's NC program management the FMS should be flexible to administer new part type redesigns in its part mix. The NC data should be neutral and transparent to the host (i.e. the host only transfers the data that is not controlled by, or does not change, the NC data). The NC Program update function should preferably not be carried out on the FMS host computer but on a CAD computer as this is a specialized function. The host should concentrate on the running of the FMS, which is another specialized function.

2. Operational flexibility
The process routings through an FMS, for a particular part type, may change due to improvement in cutting methods or routing optimization. The FMS host should have the ability to readily modify a piecepart's process routing in terms of its:

(a) operations (deletion/inclusion) on a machine type
(b) interchangeable machine tool mix for an operation
(c) sequence of operations for the interchangeable machine tool mixes

without any software changes. This should be accomplished through dialogue-driven data base modifications. After the data base has been modified, the piecepart will have a different process route with a different mix and/or sequence of interchangeable machines.

3.3.2 FMS host supplier's flexibility

This is applicable to the FMS user only in terms of the cost of the FMS host installation. The flexibility as considered by the FMS host supplier is that of the design of a suite of host software, so that a single host solution will cover most of the FMS requirements for flexibility as described above. This is not an impossible task. With the correct concept of software and host system design, most layouts and methods of application can be integrated into an FMS solution.

(a) Hardware configuration
The computer's peripheral hardware, supplied with the host, needs to be configurable into the many types of FMS layout. The FMS user should not be restricted to a particular host supplier's configuration (e.g. one VDU and two printers only) or to a specific machine tool supplier's machine design. The host should be able to interface to several designs of machine tool so that the FMS user can be free to decide which machine type to purchase according to his process requirements.

(b) A parameterizable data base
The FMS host software configuration should be parameterizable for the FMS host supplier to generate the specific system-layout (logical) data base. This is possible if the host can handle the types of constant data as shown in Figure 3.2.

The physical layout does not concern the host. The layout is decided by the part-mix, the capacities required and necessary processes. For example, a configuration might be as shown in Table 3.6.

The logical data base is parameterized through user dialogues. It is here that the different types and quantities of equipment are established for the host. For example, whether the transport system is of the random or addressable type (i.e. AGV/RGV or loop conveyor, respectively), should be transparent to the host. The host organizes transport orders for the transport system to carry out under its own control.

In this way software changes, or software creation, are avoided for the host supplier. A standardized, general-purpose, FMS function software suite can then process the parameterized data base. This approach minimizes costs for the FMS user and supplier alike.

(c) Parameterizable user-configured functions
The tactical and strategic use of the FMS, using the given data base, should also be parameterizable. This will keep the FMS user's application of the FMS independent from the host supplier's FMS software. The daily operations of running an FMS should be carried out using

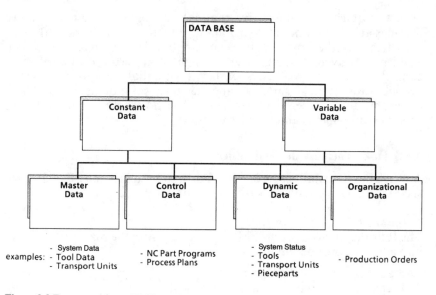

Figure 3.2 Data types in an FMS

Table 3.6 An example of an FMS configuration

Primary equipment
- work centres   2 × 5-axis universal machines
                  3 × 4-axis machining centres
                  2 × 4-axis turning centres
                  1 × head-changer

- process centres 1 × washing machine
                  1 × coordinate measuring machine

Secondary equipment
- support equipment 4 × 6-axis (hydraulic) load/unload robots
                    1 × raw-material store (stacker crane)
                    1 × pallet/fixture store
                    1 × transport system (AGVs)

- support stations 4 × manual workstations
                    1 × tool-setting machine

dialogues with screen masks for the host–human interface functions. For example, the process routings are created or modified by the operator. Their choice of piecepart route decides whether FMS is 'dedicated' (long-term fixed and known part-mix) or 'random' (unknown future part-mix). This is also true for whether the operator's instantaneous flexibility will be 'potential' (routings fixed until a machine breakdown occurs, requiring an alternative routing) or 'actual' (where alternative routings are used randomly to maintain better machine utilization).

In this way the host supplier can supply a level of flexibility which enables it to avoid forcing a rigid design or application of FMS host control on to the FMS users. A larger potential host user market is available to the host supplier, and the host solution is relevant and applicable to the user's requirements. The host solution must fit the process requirements and not vice versa.

3.3.3 How to achieve the flexibilities

All the above flexibilities have been shown to be achievable. Examples of successful FMS installations are shown in Chapter 9.

(a) FMS host operations
The four major steps for an FMS host to organize the machining system into a flexible production unit are:

1. Planning of production orders
2. Preparation of manufacturing equipment
3. Manufacturing control of the FMS
4. Monitoring of the system and equipment.

If the first two activities can be carried out parallel to the second two there will be no interruption of production.

1. (a) input of production orders
   (b) planning the capacity for the orders to be produced
   (c) establishing pallet/fixture requirements
   (d) establishing tool type and quantity requirements.
2. The preparation activities involve:
   (a) tool preparation (assembly, setting, commissioning, transfer, exchange and offset provision)
   (b) transport unit preparation (pallet/fixture build)
   (c) workpiece provision/loading–unloading.
3. Manufacturing control includes:
   (a) material flow control
   (b) NC program provision (DNC)
   (c) pallet offset provision.
4. The monitoring activities cover:
   (a) equipment status (work (machining and turning), process centres, and support and peripheral equipment)
   (b) production status (production orders and equipment utilization).

(b) Achieving instantaneous and immediate flexibility
The first two groups of activities (planning and preparation) should be run as background operations, i.e. off-line programs which are inactive and run only after they have been started by an operator. They should be decoupled from the controllers of the FMS equipment so that when they

are activated they can run without disturbing the current production activities and the on-line programs that organize these activities.

The second two groups of activities should be controlled by on-line programs which are active (i.e. always running) and in dialogue (i.e. coupled) with the controllers of the machine tools.

The operator should be able to reject the results of a planning session as often as necessary during the process of finding an acceptable result, in terms of planned equipment and capacity requirements. When accepted, the on-line material flow program can take over the results and schedule a particular piecepart to an allocated machine tool at the very last moment. Thus if a machine breaks down parts will not have been scheduled (i.e. dedicated) to it and can be re-routed to other machines of the interchangeable mix.

Instantaneous and immediate flexibility are possible when the capacity planning of the FMS is carried out 'decoupled' from the real-time functions of the host. The planning can be carried out on the same hardware parallel to the running of the on-line functions such as the material flow, machine tool control or DNC programs.

(c)   Short-term, long-term and implementation flexibilities
Short-term, long-term and implementation flexibilities are possible if the host has a data-base management system where the different types of data are managed in a way suitable to their data types. Such data can be either constant or variable according to the function for which they are used. Specific data are used to control operations and others to organize the tasks in the FMS (Figure 3.2). If the data can be updated or changed the application of the FMS host can migrate to future requirements of the FMS by the FMS user.

Constant and variable (organizational) data are only modifiable off-line from the on-line activities of the host by the operators. Variable (dynamic) data are automatically modified by the host in real time. A clear definition of a datum's type, and its subsequent correct administration, enables an FMS user to achieve the required flexibilities for the application of their FMS.

3.3.4 Productivity

The highest-cost item in an FMS is the primary equipment (e.g. the machine tools). The major object of the host should be to maximize the utilization of this equipment. This can be measured by the percentage time the spindle is cutting metal or the times that NC programs run (Figure 3.3). The secondary equipment should be underutilized so as to support the aim to achieve the maximum utilization of the primary equipment.

The FMS host enables a productivity level of that approaching transfer lines and equal to that of flexible transfer lines. This is possible as the host organizes the preparatory work to be carried out whilst a live production order mix is carried out simultaneously as a machine cuts

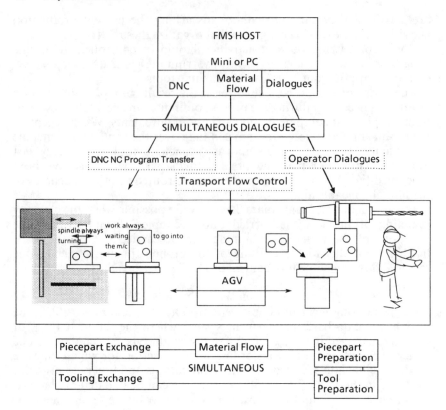

Figure 3.3 How an FMS host supports high productivity

metal, includes NC program provision (DNC), tool administration (planning, commissioning, setting, exchange), piecepart transport-unit set-up (pallets/fixtures), piecepart loading to transport units and piece-part loading to machines.

The continual supply of work to the machines' spindles provides uninterrupted production. One hundred percent metal-cutting pro-ductivity is not possible (as is also true with transfer lines, whether flexible or not), due to piecepart transfer cycles.

A drop in FMS productivity is due to NC program tool exchanges (spindle stops), tool magazine exchanges (on some designs of machine tool), piecepart change-over and non-cutting spindle movements within an NC program. The physical construction of the machine tool has a great effect on the maximum productivity achievable for that machine. Internal machine buffers for pallets loaded with work, i.e. buffers which are physically part of the machine, ensure a constant supply of work to the spindle provided the host has organized the work to be transported to these buffers. This keeps the spindle cutting as much as possible. It is the host's task to organize the supply of work to this buffer. As soon as the buffer has the capacity for more work the machine tool's controller calls up more work from the host. The host provides the work (via the transport medium) and the means to carry out the work (tools, NC program, etc.). The sustained increase in machines' utilization reduces the unit cost of a component's manufacture (i.e. productive manufacture).

Chapter 4

How an FMS works

4.1 Functions of an FMS host computer

The chief functions of an FMS host in organizing the operation of an FMS are:

    production capacity planning
    production preparation
    manufacturing control
    administration of production data.

Table 4.1 illustrates the activities concerned with each of these functions. These functions are initiated by the operator, or run independently by the host, according to the data structure and the status of the production. An overview, shown in Figure 4.1, of the functions handled by the host for managing the FMS equipment include:

    master data
    pieceparts
    tooling
    transport units (pallets and fixtures)
    processing machines.

4.1.1 A manufacturing strategy for flexibility

A production order is an order placed on an FMS for a certain quantity of pieceparts of the same type to be manufactured by a certain time. To achieve maximum flexibility the manufacturing strategy should be to produce a mix of different orders (i.e. piecepart types) within the period planned by the operator. The planning period establishes the amount of system capacity that will be used for the production order mix. This order mix and capacity planning strategy is in contrast to the strategy of batch production found in many workshops, where the production orders are scheduled to individual machines at the planning stage. When a mix of pieceparts is produced in an FMS, the machines are highly utilized as they can call up any of the next available pieceparts, already loaded on to pallets, to process. With batch production inactive, 'holes', i.e. unused capacity, appear in a machine's production sequence. This occurs when a machine is non-productive because it is unable to call up

Table 4.1 The major FMS host functions

Integration method	Function	Use

Decoupled
Off-line, inactive background
programs
Operator-initiated
	Planning	Machining/Process
		  ● capacity
		Transport units
		  ● pallets
		  ● fixtures
		Tool requirements

	Preparation	Tool - commission
		     - setting
		     - exchange
		Transport units
		  ● setting
		  ● adjustment

Coupled
On-line, active foreground
programs
Event-drive
	DNC	NC program
		  ● supply
		  ● deletion

	Material flow	Transport orders
		  ● pallets for transfer
		  ● machines needing work
		Execution
		Acknowledgement

	Monitoring	Tool lives Machine status Order status Shift lists Utilization status Report logging

pieceparts. The pieceparts are unprepared due to inflexible process routings which permanently schedule work to a machine. Inflexible schedules do not enable alternative work to visit a machine or prepared work to visit an alternative machine when either the work, or machines, are ready to get on with the next job in the process sequence.

4.1.2 Production sequence

The overall sequence to manufacture pieceparts in an FMS consists of:

● planning
● preparation
● manufacturing
● monitoring.

(a) Planning
The planning steps taken by the operator establish the production order mix to be produced in a certain period in the FMS. This is usually carried

FMS Equipment THE MAJOR HOST ACTIVITIES	Control Data	Pieceparts	Tooling	Transport Units	Process Machines
Planning	Plan Orders Process Plans	Process Routings	Plan Tool Mix	Plan Transport Unit Demand	Establish Machine Capacity and Loading
Production Preparation	Release Orders and Process Plans	Availability Check	Set and Exchange Tools	Load– Unload Transport Units	Part Program transfer DNC
Manufacturing Control	Order Admin	Load– Unload Dialogs Fixture Admin	Tool Magazine Admin	Real– Time Scheduling	Machine Control
Monitoring	Data Synchron- ization	Status– Good Rework Scrap	Tool Lives and Breakages	Status	Status

Figure 4.1 How the FMS host organizes production equipment

out interactively and should not only consider the capacity of the system still planned to be used by the current live production order mix but also the capacity required for the new production order mix. The planning algorithm should maintain a proportional relationship between the production orders' quantities so that no single order will block production of other orders. Which piecepart of the mix is to be the next one to be machined, i.e. scheduled and sent to a machine, depends upon which pieceparts are available and a priority set in real time to maintain this proportion. The duration of a planned or live order mix depends upon the production orders' parameters. These are:

● quantity of orders
● batch sizes
● number of processes per order
● program run times
● quantity of pallet/fixtures per order.

The planning software should aim to have all production orders finish not later than a specified due date. The real-time scheduler should aim to support this goal as far as possible.

The transition between a live production order mix and the following planned mix is dynamic. As previously live production orders are completed the subsequent planned orders can start automatically. This occurs once the equipment has been prepared and the order is released. This has the important advantage that the utilization of the system will be interrupted as little as possible during the dynamic transition of production order mix change-over.

The operator should input the orders into the host or transfer the data from a planning computer on a higher CIM hierarchy level, e.g. a CAP computer. The host can then calculate the following:

- tool mix per machine tool magazine
- transport units required
- machine capacity/loading required
- part-programs required.

Physical bottle necks due to the layout of the FMS can be displayed to the operator (i.e. not enough pallets or the machine magazines are too small for the tooling required). The resulting machine loadings should then be displayed to the operator.

A good planning system will allow the operator to make changes interactively to obtain the optimum plan. Such corrections might be:

- choice of an alternative process plan for a piecepart
- modification of the current process plan for a piecepart
- selection of an alternative production order for the mix
- splitting the batch quantity size over two or more periods for a production order.

(b) Production preparation
The results of the planning process enable the equipment to be prepared. These are:

- tools for setting and loading on to the machines
- clamping of fixtures on to pallets.

As the production preparation tasks are completed for an order the operator can release the order into the FMS for manufacture. The operator should be able to choose whether the orders are urgent, normal or just stock orders. The host can then set any priorities accordingly during manufacture.

(c) Manufacturing control
The instructions from the host for the operator to load and unload piecepart to and from the fixtures take place at a piecepart load–unload station. If the fixtures can carry different piecepart types (a universal fixture) a piecepart type identifier is required in the host's instruction to the operator. The simplest manufacturing strategy occurs when fixtures can carry only one piecepart type at one time for the duration of the planned production period. Reorientation of a piecepart would require

re-set-up on to another fixture on a second pallet. Some strategies, particularly for the aerospace industry, require a more complex solution where more than one piecepart type can be simultaneously fixed to a pallet. Material flow functions are part of the real-time scheduler. This also usually includes the fixture load dialogue and machine interface control programs. The host's material flow program carries out the last-minute scheduling of a piecepart to a specific machine.

The transportation of a piecepart to one of the interchangeable machines should occur subject to the following criteria:

1. The allocation of the transport unit should follow a priority rule based on the batch due date.
2. The machining centre's current capability to machine the piecepart (i.e. the machine is running and has the correct tooling and the correct part-program).
3. The machine is able to accept the piecepart (it has a free input transfer station).

When a piecepart has been loaded at a loading station for transportation to a machine tool when no machines are available to receive it, it should be displaced to a buffer station in the system. Otherwise the loading station will block the material flow for the rest of the FMS.

(d) Manual manufacturing
A machine tool has to be taken out of its normal FMS automatic mode for an operator to safely measure pallet offsets or test a part program. This manual operation of a machine, without the organizational support of the host, should be able to be carried out whilst the other machines in the system are still in full automatic FMS mode.

Pieceparts are transported with host-generated instructions to the transport system controller. The operator, however, instructs the host as to which pallets are to be transported to the machine in this manual mode. The machine should still be able to receive, via the DNC link, the necessary part programs. Transmission can be initiated by the operator at the NC's control panel.

(e) Monitoring
The machine tools in the FMS should be continuously monitored by the host so that it is always updated with the changing status of the FMS. If a machine breaks down the CNC should send an alarm to the host so that no work will be supplied to that machine. The host should periodically request a status check from the machine so that, if the machine cannot send an alarm telegram, the machine's not answering would mean to the host that it has broken down.

The CNC monitors the tooling in the machine's magazine, the peripheral equipment and the current piecepart the machine is working upon. Their changing status should also be reported to the host:

● machine status
● tool lives

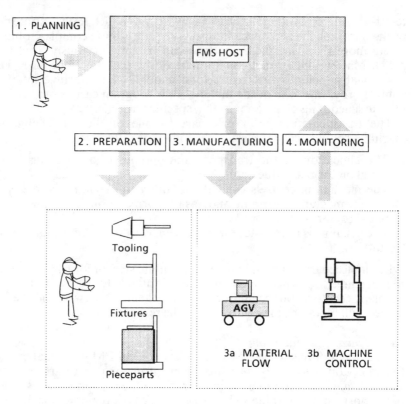

Figure 4.2 The four operations in a functioning FMS

- cutting abnormalities
- tool breakages
- error diagnostics.

In this way the host is always synchronized logically with what is physically happening in the FMS. Figure 4.2 summarizes pictorially these four operations to run an FMS.

4.2 How an FMS host is integrated into an FMS

An FMS consists of computers and controllers. The host is only one computer in this mix of computers and controllers configured into an FMS. Each computer must interface to the others in the CIM hierarchy for transfer of data upon which the computers carry out their functions (Figure 4.3).

To achieve successful continuity of data exchange the interfaces must

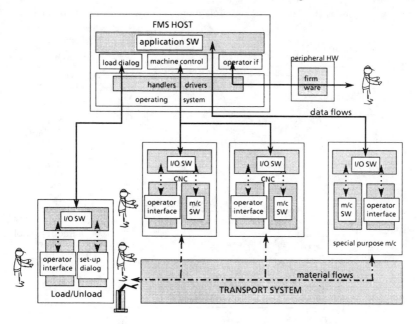

Figure 4.3 The communication interfaces in an FMS

be specified on the following levels:

1. Physical   – links (serial, parallel, Centronics, etc.)
               – networks (LAN/backbone/WAN)
               – handshakes (infra-red, inductance, hardwired)
2. Logical   – protocols (ISO/OSI, TCP/IP/MAP/Ethernet/token
                 ring/pass/etc.)
               – procedures (telegram sequences, etc.)
3. Functional – tasks (application software, etc.).

Until an international standard is agreed and accepted by industry the CIM concept is heavily dependent upon proprietary solutions for the physical and logical solution for an interface. The functional aspects will always be proprietary for as long as FMS suppliers wish to provide FMS solutions. When the means for transferring data are established, whatever the solution, a functional integration can be implemented.

Whether the data transfer is a file transfer or a transaction (program to program) a dialogue is required between two controllers (Figure 4.4). The dialogue involves a sequence of telegrams to be exchanged in a specific sequence. A telegram is sent as a result of a specific cause at the sending controller (e.g. the request for a tool-life update from the slave controller in the dialogue). The arrival of a telegram has an effect at the receiving controller (e.g. seek tool life and transmit to master controller

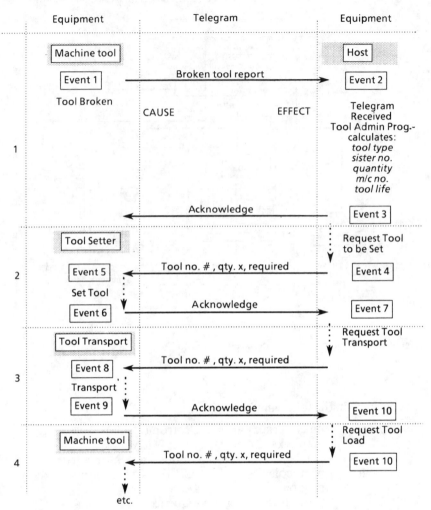

Figure 4.4 Example of an interface dialogue

in the dialogue). Each telegram has a specific function, and thus an interface description/specification should describe:

● telegrams' formats (header, user data, trailers)
● causes
● effects
● sequence.

When the specification is clear and unambiguous, software can be created for both controllers to drive and handle the dialogues and execute the functions successfully.

4.2.1 Functional requirements of the FMS equipment

(a) Work-centre functions
Work centres, such as machining centres or turning centres, are purchased to cut metal. They earn money whilst the spindle turns, cutting
metal and adding value to a piecepart; they cost money when the spindle
is not turning. To improve the utilization of the spindle and therefore the
productivity of the work centre, a computer numerical controller (CNC)
is integrated on to the machine. The CNC's task is to control the process,
i.e. spindle movement. CNCs are often constructed as an NC unit
integrated with a programmable logic controller (PLC) and even an
additional external PLC (non-integrated). The NC controls the geometry
of the spindle's movements and the speeds and feeds of the cutters. The
PLC(s) control the peripheral equipment of the machine (component
exchange on the turntable, tool magazine, oil coolant system, hand-
shakes and host dialogues, etc.).

Working together, the NC and PLCs enable the work centre to operate
as an autonomous stand-alone machine.

(b) Process-centre functions
The functions of a process centre depend upon the process to be
controlled, for example wash, measure, assemble, etc. Usually only a
PLC is installed where no precise spindle/cutter control is needed. The
exception is where piecepart measurement is required. For this process a
minicomputer is often needed to provide the solution. The process is
sequenced, controlled and monitored by the PLC, which also executes
any dialogue and handshake functions required.

(c) Secondary equipment functions
Usually secondary equipment does not have any control function
requirements. It mechanically performs 'dumb' functions such as the
buffer storage of pieceparts (inactive) or reacts to host dialogue instructions (active), as with a manual workstation that has an instruction
terminal. They do not control any processes through a control loop: for
example, a terminal at the component load/unload station requires the
operator to carry out the instructions.

4.2.2 Machining centre dialogues and functions

By way of an example, the requirements for a machining centre's
dialogue functions are analysed to illustrate the complex dialogues
needed to integrate such a work centre into an FMS. Various dialogues
are conducted to support the functions for which the machining centre is
responsible. These dialogues are carried out with:

● the host
● the other level 2 equipment (e.g. AGVs)
● the operators.

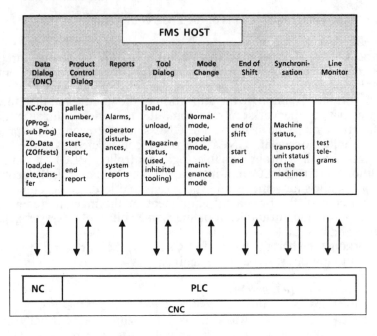

FMS HOST							
Data Dialog (DNC)	Product Control Dialog	Reports	Tool Dialog	Mode Change	End of Shift	Synchroni- sation	Line Monitor
NC-Prog (PProg, sub Prog) ZO-Data (ZOffsets) load,del- ete,trans- fer	pallet number, release, start report, end report	Alarms, operator disturb- ances, system reports	load, unload, Magazine status, (used, inhibited tooling)	Normal- mode, special mode, maint- enance mode	end of shift start end	Machine status, transport unit status on the machines	test tele- grams

NC	PLC
CNC	

Figure 4.5 Host interface to the CNC

Figure 4.5 illustrates the relationship between the controllers and the dialogues and functions which are carried out.

(a) Data dialogue
The distributed numerical control (DNC) function of down- and up-loading the NC programs is carried out between the host and the NC. The NC program includes any administration data block, the part-program itself, the tool plans, sub-programs and the NC routines. The NC stores all but the administration data block. Pallet offset measurement data are also down-loaded.

This dialogue also enables and permits the NC to delete and return-transmit the part-programs and tool plans.

(b) Production dialogue
To enable organization of production, the machining centre must report the pallet identity of the pallet which has just been delivered to it. The host can then check if it is a correct pallet for which the part-program may be down-loaded and if the tool set in the magazine corresponds to the part-program.

If the correct pallet has been delivered with the correct piecepart, and all the production equipment is available, the host can then provide permission for the CNC to start machining. The responsibility to start machining remains with the CNC, which has other machine-specific criteria to consider before the safe cutting of metal may commence (e.g. piecepart safely positioned in the machine's work area).

The CNC reports the start of a part-program and the successful conclusion of the program run. With these data the host can maintain the current status of that particular machine tool (in-process, idle or in-dialogue).

(c) Report functions
If an event-driven status change occurs (planned or unplanned) the CNC must report this to the host. If this is carried out the host can maintain the current status of the machine and react to the change if necessary. The reports can either be

● alarms or
● system messages

Alarms are status changes that either mean the machine has stopped working, as it would be dangerous for it to continue to do so, or, if the cause is not so drastic, it will stop as soon as the current part-program is completed. The host should subsequently inform the FMS manager and cease the organization of the supply of work to the particular machine.

System messages are reports warning of a status on the machine that may lead to an alarm. They are issued for an operator to take preventive action (e.g. when the oil pressure is low). They may also consist purely of information data upon which the host can base statistical analyses. The reports need not only be for alarms or statistical data. They may also arise merely to inform the FMS manager of an event occurring to which the host is parameterized to take no action whatsoever. For example a report should be sent to the host when a machine operator has manually interrupted the running of a part's program.

(d) Tool dialogue
The PLC of the CNC administers the tool magazine on the machine tool. Dialogues are carried out with the host when tools are exchanged (loaded and unloaded). The exchange activity is conducted between the machine operator (or robot) and the PLC. Once they have been loaded, the new tool data, i.e. which tools were loaded, are sent to the host. The host administers a logical picture of the magazine's status. The host should be able to request an update of all the tools in the magazine status or just those which were exchanged. When the host knows which tools are in the magazine it can down-load the tool offsets, which have previously been sent to the host from a tool-setting machine, in a tool-setting dialogue.

The host also needs to know which 'inhibited' tools are in the magazine so as to have a true picture of how many physical tool locations are available for tool exchanges. This is necessary when planning work for the machine which gives rise to a specific tool requirement for the machine. Inhibited tools are those tools that have been loaded manually without any tool planning having been carried out on the host.

(e) Mode changing
A machine tool can work in various modes to the host. These are:

● automatic
● DNC
● maintenance
● stand-alone.

Automatic mode is the normal operational mode between the machine and a host. The host organizes the production activities for the machine and monitors its status. The host instructs the transport system controller to send work to the machine. The machine will not know the sequence of piecepart types which will visit the machine. The machine is totally dependent on the host to be brought into a status so that the machine can process the work as it arrives.

DNC mode includes a subset of the automatic mode functions. Any DNC operation should be initiated at the NC's panel by an operator. The operator can call down the part programs they require from the host. They should also be able to initiate the transportation of components to the machine. The instruction to the transport controller should still come from the host but not be created automatically when in this mode. The machine in DNC mode should not be included in any production planning that the host may carry out for other machines. This planning inhibition should occur as soon as the relevant machine has been switched into DNC mode. The mode switching is to be carried out by the FMS manager using a terminal dialogue at the host (probably at a VDU).

Maintenance mode is similar to DNC mode. However, no manually generated transportation of pieceparts should be possible. The machine is switched into this mode when it is expected to be out of operation for a long period. This usually occurs when certain equipment has broken down and cannot transfer components on to the machine anyway. If the CNC is not working it will not be capable of receiving or transmitting NC programs. The mode is used for the host to be aware of the latest status of a machine. The mode may also be used when the maintenance is planned, whether the machine or its controller has broken down or not. The host needs to be aware of the decreased capacity in the FMS which has to be taken into account in any planning carried out in the meantime. The mode should be initiated at the host.

Stand-alone mode is the same status between a machine and the host as if the connection to the host has been physically cut. The machine is unsynchronized with the host. The host should ignore the machine completely as if it were not configured into the layout of the FMS. This mode is useful during commissioning of an FMS. If the machine's interface has been successfully integrated into the FMS the machine can be used to produce pieceparts without interrupting the tests (and vice versa) on the other machine interfaces in the FMS.

(f) End-of-shift function

If a non-productive period occurs, e.g. between shifts, the machines should be switched off into a known safe status. The safest status is achieved when no pieceparts are left in the machines' work area. The pallets in the FMS should be transferred to buffer stores or allowed to remain on any internal buffer storage in the work stations. When this is achieved any unplanned maintenance occurring during the non-productive period can commence with the machines being started in a safe status. This is also true for start-up on the next shift.

This function, initiated at the host, is not always used. In some systems the operators cease to load up the FMS with work at the piecepart load/unload stations. This leads to the machines running out of work. The FMS slows to a stop and ends up in a similar status to that had the function been used. When this method, or the original function, is used the CNCs must ensure that the spindle areas are cleared of work. However, the contents of the FMS may run down if the system does not continue to be loaded with work until the safe-mode status is reached, which will prevent the loading of any further work into the FMS. If this is not carried out it will require costly time to load up to the system's capacity again.

At the end of the requirement for this mode the FMS can be switched back into automatic or DNC mode.

(g) Synchronization

In automatic mode the host always knows the status of the machine. If a machine is ever taken out of automatic mode the logical status image of the machine in the host must always be updated. This is true even if there have been no manual operations carried out at the machine and the status has remained the same.

The host needs to know if there are any outstanding alarms, which NC programs are in the NC's memory, which tools are in the magazine and which pallets/pieceparts (if any) are in the machine. The tool update can be carried out with the normal tool dialogue if required. When synchronized the machine can be put back into the automatic mode.

(h) Line-check function

A telegram can be sent from, and returned to, the host to check that the physical connection is still in operation. When NC program run times of 30 min to several hours occur there may be no communication between the host and the machine for quite lengthy periods. This could also be due to a line breakdown, however. To avoid a broken down machine being ignored, due to a wrong assumption, line check telegrams should be sent periodically. The intervals between telegram initiation should be parameterizable.

(i) Operation of dialogues

The dialogues described are all bidirectional except for the report telegrams. These are only sent to the host. It is not enough to have functioning dialogue software in the host and CNC. Once the dialogues are successfully concluded, the information received must be acted upon by the function software.

4.2.3 Host system design

The FMS host computer involves a lot of complex software to be able to administer all the data received from level 2 and 4 computers. The host may have to execute dialogues with up to 30 interfaces in a large FMS, including transactions with area computers on level 4. The types of software required to run (not create) an FMS are:

1. System software:
    - (a) operating system
    - (b) data-base management
    - (c) dialogue/display/reporting packages
    - (d) libraries/routines/utilities
    - (e) graphics
    - (f) software buses/communication packages
    - (g) drivers/handlers
    - (h) interrupt handler.
2. FMS software – standard proprietary FMS functions.
3. FMS application software – software to tailor the FMS software to a particular FMS's design requirements.

(a) System software
System software is required for any computer system. For an FMS host the real-time characteristics demand that the correct system software is selected on the correct hardware with which to develop the FMS host system. Small systems with two or three machining centres and long NC program run times may only necessitate an FMC host hardware environment based on the smaller capacity of a personal computer. Systems with eight machines, short processing times and complex FMS software requirements will need a processing minicomputer which can handle a multitude of interfaces/interrupts and handle them on a priority basis.

Most FMSs require multi-tasking, multi-user operating systems which are able to work in a real-time on-line environment of the factory's shop floor.

(b) Standard FMS software functions
There is a common requirement for data management and functions in all FMSs. The FMS software works with a data base, which is initially input by the FMS manager and then continually updated by the data transactions through the interfaces to the controllers on the other levels.

Data base. The data base consists of different types of data. The data (Figure 3.2) administered by the host includes:

1. Constant data. These are data which do not and may not be changed, even as a result of the host accessing them.
   (a) Master data (data which describe the system or physical units within the system).
   (b) Control data (data which control a process).
2. Variable data. These are data which change as the FMS carries out its functions.
   (a) Dynamic data (data which describe the changing status of the units in the FMS).
   (b) Organizational data (different data used to plan work in the FMS).

Program types. The FMS software programs are either 'coupled' or 'decoupled' from the machines and their controllers. Coupled programs are continuously active and control the data transactions with the level 2 controllers or terminals. The decoupled programs process the data in the data base. They are not in direct contact with the data traffic between the host, machine controllers or shop-floor operators. They are only active when the operator at the host initiates them.

Dialogue systems. A host transacts the following types of dialogue:

1. Operator to host
2. Host's program to program
3. Host's programs to data base
4. Host to/from level 2 controllers (CNCs, PLCs, etc.)
5. Host to/from level 3 and/or 4 controllers (computers, etc.)
6. Host to operator.

For (1) a VDU or terminal menu mask system is required. For (2) and (3) a software communications bus system is necessary. Specific handlers and drivers are used for (4) and (5). For (6) a standard reporting system can be used. These systems are usually standard packages for use in computer systems, whether FMS or not.

4.2.4 FMS host function requirements

The host needs to be able to carry out a minimum set of FMS functions if the full benefits of FMS are to be gained in a production system. These are illustrated in Figure 4.6. Examples of functions and modules that are required to drive a sophisticated FMS are described, along with the data base requirements, to illustrate the complexity of an FMS host.

(a) Data base
Works calendar. The available productive time, within which a host can base its planning, needs to be realistic. This should be parameterizable to adapt to changes in shift times over the years or between different workshops/factories.

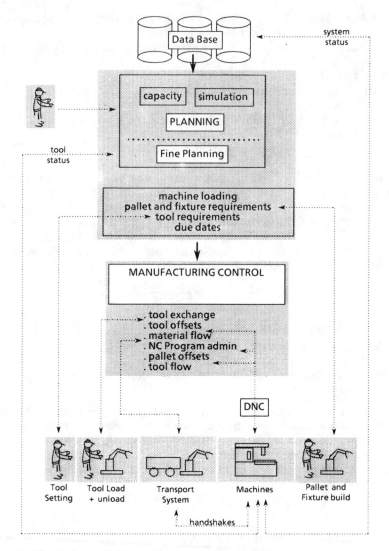

Figure 4.6 The minimum FMS host functions/dialogues

Tool data. All tooling in the FMS requires describing logically in the host's data banks. The data base should be able to cater for all types of tools (single- or multi-spindle, single- or multi-tipped, etc.)

NC programs. The storage of NC programs should cater for at least the standard types of coding (EIA, ISO, ASCII).

Process plans. There should be a plan for every piecepart to be produced in the FMS which determines the machines upon which they can be manufactured. The process plans should allow all workstations in the FMS to be allocated to pieceparts operations either interchangeably or complementarily. 'Alternative' process plans will ensure that any bottle-neck machines that break down do not block the production of some or all of the pieceparts which use the process plans containing the bottle-neck machines.

Pallets/Fixtures. The equipment which is used to carry pieceparts in an FMS requires a logical description in the host's data banks. Each pallet and fixture is administered by its master data. When they are clamped together they form a logical 'transport unit' which the host also administers.

System layout. The layout and configuration of the FMS which the host is to control also requires a logical description.

Production orders. A production order describes how many of which type of piecepart to manufacture. It also indicates the due date by which the order should be ready.

(b) Decoupled functions

Planning. The capacity of the FMS needs planning for a specific mix of pieceparts to be produced in a given period. This planning function is carried out parallel to the manufacture of a previously planned piecepart mix. The planning can be pure capacity planning only, with the alloca-tion of actual pieceparts to a particular machine being carried out at the last moment by a coupled material flow program. Or it can be a simulation of the material flow with the pieceparts being 'logically' scheduled to specific machines before the material flow takes over the plan and sends the pieceparts to the scheduled machines. The former method is more flexible. If in real time a machine breaks down the pieceparts which would have gone to this machine are still free to be allocated to the alternative machines in the interchangeable mix of machines allocated for the piecepart's operation. A simulation is only accurate as long as there are no disturbances in the FMS in real time. As soon as a machine breaks down the simulation must be carried out again.

A capacity planning module can calculate the due date for the planned mix of pieceparts only. A simulated plan can give due dates for each piecepart type (production order) in the mix, whether accurate or not. It is for the FMS user to decide which type of planning they require.

The output of the planning should be:

● machine loading
● pallet/fixture requirements
● tool types needed
● due date(s).

Tool planning. Subsequent to the production order planning, a more accurate tool planning function is necessary. This considers the tool types required for the production order mix planned and calculates the true number of each tool type needed in each machine tool magazine. The tools already in the magazine must be considered so as not to plan too many tools. Tool lives must be considered in order to establish the quantity of complementary tools needed.

Tool setting. The planned tools need setting for their tool offsets to be measured. These offsets are subsequently transferred to the NC of a particular machine tool via the host, bar code or by a read/write chip on the tool shank itself.

System status. The host needs to know the status of the FMS (machines, production orders, equipment, etc.) A collection of programs will enable shift lists, tool lists, machine utilization statistics lists, etc., to be generated based on the status information. A system mimic picture (an animated automatically updated pictorial layout of the FMS, on a colour VDU) can also be generated from the system status data.

Special operations. Special operations are necessary to assist normal automatic operation of the FMS. They are needed to initially load production into an FMS, or when disturbances occur. These may include manually directing transport units to any transfer station (e.g. set-up or service areas), changing the mode of a machine tool (e.g. DNC or off-line), selecting the end-of-shift function or resynchronizing the system.

(c) Coupled functions
Component load/unload dialogue. A program is required to instruct the shop-floor operator(s) which piecepart(s) to set up and/or down. The instructions are relevant for the transport units which arrive at the load/unload station. Declarations of piecepart scrap or rework should be possible to update the status of the piecepart to the host. The setter acknowledges the completion of the host-driven task at a terminal. The host can then organize the collection of the transport unit for delivery to a machine or buffer station. Some systems include an inspection activity in the dialogue, either at the load/unload station or at a station dedicated to inspection.

Tool load/unload dialogue. Tool exchange can be planned or unplanned. Depending upon which, the dialogue can also be host-driven or manually driven. Whichever combination of dialogue is used, the host is required to down-load any tool offsets and be updated to the new machine-tool magazine status.

Material flow. This is the most important function. Without this function the system can only ever be a DNC system and not an FMS. This module instructs the transport system controller to transfer a pallet (with or without piecepart) around the FMS. The material flow module marries the requirements of machines calling for work to transport units ready for transfer. The result is a transport order for the transport system controller to carry out. A displacement strategy is necessary for the frequent situations when several transport units are only able to be transported at one time. This may simply be to a FIFO rule or to a set list of priority rules.

An example of transport priorities is as follows (top to bottom priority):

- machine to load/unload area (a priority can be set between work-stations and process stations)
- machine to buffer
- load/unload area to machine
- load/unload area to buffer
- buffer to buffer (should never happen in a well-laid-out, balanced FMS).

Some simple systems rely upon an exchange strategy where pallets travel to and from the same machine tool and load/unload station to process the piecepart. A more flexible solution is where a pallet can be displaced to a buffer to allow other pallets to travel to the machine tool or load/unload station. This prevents bottle-necks occurring when a particular pallet, with its piecepart, is not yet ready to be transferred but another pallet is ready. An even more flexible solution is when the pallet can go to one of a mix of interchangeable (alternative) machines or load/unload stations.

Machine control. A module is required to monitor the work station(s) and administer the level 2 and 3 controller dialogues. This module acts as coordinator to several other modules which are responsible for supplying the work centres with data. The status of each machine is also maintained with this module. Alarms from the machines are captured and sent to the relevant host module for action. A requirement to down-load an NC program will be noted and the necessary action passed on to a DNC module. The module administers a logical image of the NC program loading of each NC memory for which the module is responsible.

DNC. Upon instruction from a machine control module the DNC module will down-load the required NC program(s). This module is not required for FMSs where the NC program lengths enable all programs to fit into the CNCs' memories. This is unusual and may affect the FMS's long-term flexibility. The module should have the capability to handle part-programs, sub-programs and tool plans. Drip-feeding of programs may be necessary for very long programs, such as for contouring operations where the program may be 5 Mbytes long.

Tool magazine administration. Another module which works with the machine control module is the module which administers a logical image of all the tool magazines on all the work centres. This assists tool planning, preventing costly duplication of tooling or overloading of magazines. Tools in the magazines and their tool lives can therefore be administered by the host.

Simulation. Modules to simulate workstations and transport systems assist FMS commissioning and are also used in a normal running FMS to support the planning operation.

Tool flow control. Total tool administration includes:

● tool component store administration
● tool planning
● tool (de-)commissioning (disassembly/assembly)
● tool transportation (manual or automatic)
● tool load/unload
● tool monitoring.

It is not always the case that the tool-storage, commissioning and automatic transportation functions are installed to their fullest extent due to the high costs involved in the hardware (tooling, robots, gantrys, AGVs, stores, etc.). An FMS host should, however, have the software to cater for these functions. Automatic tool flow is becoming more wide-spread as the various machine tool builders develop their own solutions. Tool transportation can be on the back of pallets, or plattens, in groups for a particular magazine, for example, or the tools might be transferrerd individually, by a gantry robot, for example. The transfer may occur before a production period is started or as a piecepart arrives at a machine. The method depends upon piecepart size, tool requirement per piecepart, NC program run time and the size of the tools. Thus the tool automation method is very much dependent upon the FMS user and the piecepart mix that they plan to manufacture in the FMS.

(d) Miscellaneous functions
Various functions make an FMS host user-friendly or safe to use:

Password administration. This function allows only authorized person-nel to access the data base and process the data using the FMS software. The FMS user should be able to parameterize who can use which functions.

Data security. Several levels of securing data bases, and therefore production running, are possible:

● copying the data base with off-site storage
● parallel data-writing to two disc drives (with manual or automatic switch-over when one disc goes down)
● cold or hot stand-by host (with manual or automatic switch-over when the slave host goes down).

The selection of security level is a function of cost of FMS host against the costs of decreased production due to stand-alone operation when the host breaks down. A personal computer solution will not be able to offer all the security options that a minicomputer can.

Cold/warm-start options. This level of user-friendliness will depend upon the choice of FMS host hardware and software selected.

Menu-mask operation. All FMS solutions should provide a user-friendly mask operation. To manage an FMS is difficult enough without having to use solution-specific commands. 'Window' mask operation is beginning to be used more frequently as a solution.

Logging and error reports. All events should be logged for any post-mortem analyses. Alarm messages should be printed out immediately and logged. Non-critical messages should be printed and/or logged for reporting later.

4.3 FMS host and area controller function distribution

As a computer has only a finite capacity it may be required to distribute the FMS host functions over several units of hardware. When an FMS is particularly large, or has unusually high performance requirements, an FMS level 3(b) master host can be installed above several level 3(a) FMS hosts. An area controller on level 4 can be installed above the master host. Some of the FMS host functions are passed on to the FMS master host. It will depend on the total system design whether the functions removed from the FMS host can be switched back on if the master host breaks down. A standby host can be provided, for large multi-FMS systems, which can take over a broken-down level 3 or 4 host's tasks (hardware replacement).

Certain functions will be centralized and controlled at the master host computer. Others will be duplicated across the subordinate FMS host systems. Certain functions have to be performed at both levels of control.

In large systems, where several machine-tool types may be installed, it is often easier to install a subordinate host over each type of machine. This will simplify the interfaces on each host. In such a system a master host may be required to coordinate all the cells in the system.

4.3.1 FMS master host tasks

The tasks that the master host computer can perform are:

● production order planning
● tool planning
● level 3 hosts' status monitoring

- NC program administration
- system image mimic picture
- tool setting (if centralized)
- material flow (if centralized)
- system shift/utilization lists
- connection to any level 4 or 5 computer(s).

4.3.2 Subordinate FMS host tasks

The following tasks are those which are essential to an FMS host to organize the production of a group of work centres and cannot be displaced to a coordinating master host:

- material flow
- tool flow
- machine control
- NC program administration
- tool load/unload dialogue
- component load/unload dialogue
- system/alarm report monitoring
- system image mimic picture (subsystem specific)
- synchronization.

4.3.3 Area controller host tasks

The area controller plans the work to go into a manufacturing area's available capacity and may even provide the transport organization to physically arrange that the area's production facilities are provided with work. These facilities may well be one or several FMSs. Either an FMS host or master host will interface to the area controller or corporate computer level. The data exchange carried out is to update the FMS hosts with new data bases or to inform the corporate computers of the status of the FMSs. The data exchanges (Figure 4.7) are:

NC programs. NC programs created on CAD systems can be transferred to the host's data base or returned to the CAD's data base, after modification at the CNC level, for instance. Transfer would be for administration data blocks, part-programs, sub-programs, routines, tool plans and program lists.

Production orders. New production orders can be sent to the FMS host's production order pool, for manufacturing, or the status of those already sent can be returned to the level 4 or 5 CAP computer.

Master data. The level 4 or 5 computer may hold a complete factory data base of which the FMS's data base is only a subset. The FMS's data base will need updating if the corporate data base is updated. The updates would include tool, pallet, fixture and system parameter constant data.

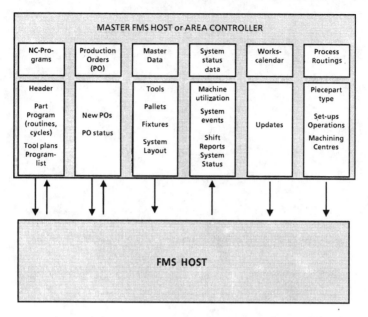

Figure 4.7 The host interface to a master FMS host or area controller

System status data. A CAP computer on level 5 needs to know the status of an FMS, and other production equipment, to carry out a factory-wide capacity plan. Such a computer would receive machine utilization statistics, system events, shift data and equipment status data from the host.

Works calendar. If shift hours should change, the hosts would require updating to perform realistic capacity planning.

Process routings. New process routings would need transferring to the relevant hosts should manufacturing methods be modified for a piece-part. Such information would include part number, fixture identification, operations (NC programs) and work centres.

Chapter 5

How to develop your FMS

If FMS technology seems to be suitable for a company's production requirements there are various steps to go through to analyse and design the most appropriate FMS solution.

5.1 Planning phases

There are four major phases that an FMS user goes through to implement his FMS. These are the:

1. Awareness phase
2. Planning phase
3. Installation phase
4. Operation phase.

These phases are shown in Figure 5.1 and are common to all projects. As FMS is a growing technology even some of the 'experts' and suppliers are still on the learning curve. At each phase controls, checks and decisions need to be made before passing on to the next phase.

5.1.1 Awareness phase – what can an FMS do?

To be fully aware of what an FMS can do for a company the potential FMS user must accumulate knowledge on a general level in order to communicate competently with expert FMS suppliers. This knowledge can be obtained at reference sites of FMS suppliers, seminars, conferences, books, published articles and from the FMS suppliers themselves. The potential FMS user should be completely aware of what benefits the FMS will bring them.

5.1.2 Planning phase – what should an FMS do for me?

During this phase the potential FMS user crystallizes exactly what the FMS is to do for him. To accomplish this the company should set up a project team with a project manager. A long-term FMS strategy for the whole company should be developed. Total commitment from the entire management should be obtained. The financial evaluation should be made objectively with the team identifying exactly which processes for

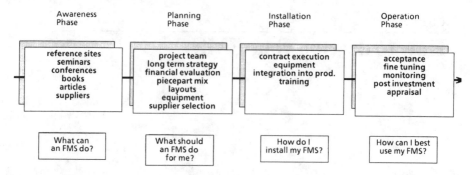

Figure 5.1 The phases to build an FMS

which pieceparts are to be contained in the FMS. The team should be aware that the FMS will affect the whole company and prepare to educate others and to make the necessary changes within the company's production environment and organization. Product, process and tooling standardization may be required. Alternative materials, FMS layouts and configurations require evaluation. When installing an FMS the system must be integrated into the factory's total operations.

An FMS can be likened to a road system. When a traffic jam in town occurs a bypass dual-carriageway is often constructed. This eases the problem in town but can just pass the traffic jam problem to the next town if a total traffic scheme is not planned (e.g. a motorway bypassing the whole area). This can also be the case in a factory. Why install an effective, efficient FMS when older supply systems in other departments cannot keep up with the new throughput rate? Why increase the throughput rate when parts just have to sit longer in an assembly department? A total CIM and AMT policy needs to be conceptualized and planned for the whole factory.

The selection of the correct FMS supplier is critical. The following major questions should be asked of the would-be supplier:

1. Has the company got the right capabilities?
2. Are the correct processes being supplied?
3. Has the company the capacity for a one to two year project?
4. Is the company financially sound to provide support for the possible 15 year life of the FMS?
5. What standard interfaces and functions can be supplied?
6. Will the company take over the general contractor's role?
7. What support and level of training will be provided?
8. Is the correct FMS and CIM concept being supplied?
9. Can the system be expanded in a stepwise approach?

Other questions common to capital investment projects also arise but are discussed in chapter 8. The potential FMS supplier(s) should develop the FMS configuration with the FMS user company to ensure that the investment is with the most suitable FMS supplier.

5.1.3 Installation phase – how do I install my FMS?

The installation of an FMS is like a three-legged stool – take one leg away and the stool falls over. The three legs supporting the installation of an FMS are:

1. Machine tool supplier(s)
2. FMS host supplier (often the systems integration specialist)
3. FMS user.

In some cases the user is also the host and/or machine tool supplier. This would be where a machine tool builder is using his own system in an in-house FMS application. The machine tool builder may have their own FMS host solution which they can offer to a would-be user, but quite often the FMS host supplier is a separate hardware and/or system software house specializing in the subject.

The machine tool supplier has the responsibility to guarantee a specified throughput for the FMS. As a safeguard this will be for a given piecepart mix. This company can bring the production engineering experience to a project. The host supplier can bring the systems engineering experience for automation to the project. Some suppliers who provide the automation for all the levels in the CIM hierarchy also provide the integration experience. The FMS user brings the experience of how to best manufacture his pieceparts. Each party needs the other parties for the project to be a success. It is important to define, at this early stage, who the project/contract's general contractor will be. There is more than one way to organize a project (two examples are shown in Figure 5.2). It is easier for the FMS user if he ensures that the machine tool builder takes over this function.

The FMS user has the following major tasks:

1. Construction of the FMS site
2. Integration of the other departments to the FMS
3. Purchase of tooling, fixtures, etc.
4. Planning for production any stoppages during commissioning
5. Planning the test and acceptance methods suitable to all parties
6. Planning for the training and take-over activities.

5.1.4 Operation phase – how can I best use my FMS?

When the FMS is installed the FMS user is, to a large extent, left on his own. Errors occurring during a guarantee period will, of course, be solved by the relevant supplier. However, the FMS user can now learn to adjust and fine-tune the FMS to the best operating conditions, and piece-part mixes, in relation to his own criteria. The FMS user company may well wish not to run the FMS with the original piecepart mix as specified in the contractual criteria agreed by the parties in order that system acceptance could be achieved. To do this a monitoring period is required.

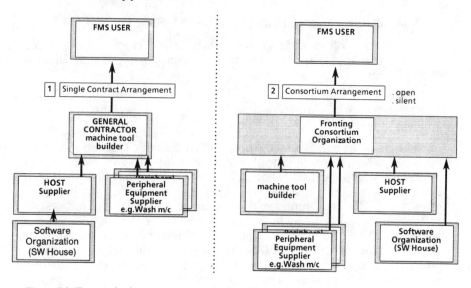

Figure 5.2 Two methods to carry out an FMS project

This also allows an opportunity for a post-investment appraisal. The major criteria to be monitored are:
- system balance (e.g. machine tool utilization)
- lead times and cycle times for processes and set-ups
- batch sizes and mixes
- stoppages (quantities and causes)
- quality
- maintenance required
- production costs
- revenues from FMS.

5.2 Integration

FMS is no longer a pioneering technology. The above phases will ensure successful implementation of FMS automation. However, it must also be integrated successfully into the total factory environment.

Over 20 years ago the original FMSs were installed as large, cumbersome, stand-alone FMS installations. The present day has seen the advent of smaller, low-cost, higher-capacity and more capable hardware with powerful system software. It is only recently, since the mid-1980s that a few supplier companies have been able to develop and supply cost-effective FMS hosts. A few companies are even in a position to supply the hosts with standard parameterizable FMS host software. Effective level 2 PLC and CNC hardware/software has been in existence for over a decade. This is also the trend for the level 5 corporate planning computer solutions. The pioneering areas of integration concern the interfaces between the factory planning computers and the CNC level of controllers. FMS hosts are slowly providing this capability.

With the arrival of effective FMS hosts the potential now exists for FMS user companies to completely automate the factory environment. Continuous data integration from levels 1 to 5 is possible. Industry has conceived such integration for years but has not fully embarked upon this route with metal-cutting FMSs. The integration must be correctly planned. FMS can be considered as another standard building block for automation providing the potential to achieve the ideals of the factory of the future (FOF).

CIM is not a 'quick-fix'. It must be correctly planned (top-down) and realistically implemented (bottom-up). There is a shortage of expertise to provide all five levels of integration, but experience is being gathered by FMS suppliers and users to make such CIM objectives achievable.

5.3 System configuration

The configuration of an FMS involves the selection of the types and quantitites of the primary and secondary equipment. The layout of an FMS decides the physical positioning of the configuration. The layout and configuration of an FMS will depend upon the piecepart mix to be produced. The number and types of machines will determine the machining capabilities and capacities for NC operations.

Maximum flexibility is achieved when all machines are configured interchangeably in the pieceparts' process routings. This requires every machine tool to have the same tool sets. This may therefore result in the duplication of certain tools and can be expensive with high training costs. Often certain machine tool groups are allocated subsets of the total piecepart mix to reduce tool duplication. This compromises the flexibility but enables lower tooling costs.

To ensure that no bottle-necks occur, with corresponding machine starvations, it is almost mandatory to simulate the alternative layouts and component-mix loadings for each particular FMS configuration. The objective is to optimize the layout prior to embarking on any irretrievable capital expenditure.

The layout and configuration of an FMS involves a great amount of production engineering experience. The responsibility of the layout is that of the FMS supplier. This is usually the machine tool builder, who often acts as the general contractor. The major financial and techno-logical risk is concerned with the correct capital equipment, with the correct configuration and layout, being chosen. The organization of production for the machine tools is the responsibility of the FMS host from the host supplier. The host usually constitutes only 10–20% of the total project's costs. For this reason host suppliers do not readily accept the role of general contractor.

The machine tools should have the capability to manufacture with and without the host supporting production. Operation without the host is often known as 'stand-alone mode'. This is required as the host may break down or require servicing. Production can still be maintained, although at a lower level of productivity, at a lower level of automation if the machines can run as autonomous production units. The more advanced FMS host can organize the production of different types of FMS configuration which may include, for example:

1. Universal machining centres with inductively guided transport systems (large variety, small part size, prismatic mix production).
2. Twin turning centre stations with localized gantry robot transportation and global inductively guided transport system (medium batch size, rotational part-mix production).
3. Linear layout of machining centres with a rail-guided transport vehicle (small variety, large part size, prismatic mix production).
4. Dissimilar machining and processing centres with host-driven manual transportation (undefined batch size, hybrid part-mix production).

Most systems have peripheral equipment such as assembly stations, fixture or material stores and tool-setting stations.

All these types of equipment, layouts and configurations can be adequately simulated today with systems that are commercially available to the potential FMS user.

5.4 FMS layouts

When a company has decided to install an FMS it establishes a machining capacity requirement for the piecepart type mix to be manufactured in the FMS. To produce this mix specific machines and processes are required. Each of these machines will have a certain capacity which, when aggregated, creates the system capacity of the FMS. Pieceparts' characteristics, such as size and weight, dictate the most suitable method of transportation between the machines, and the transfer mechanism between the machines and transport system(s). Batch quantity sizes, lead times, process times, cycle times and required throughputs will dictate the quantity of each process or machine type required. The quantity of secondary equipment will depend upon the capacities of the primary equipment: for example, 20 buffer stations to support the material flow for 15 machining centres and two load/unload stations.

5.5 Simulation

A compromise between the ideal system capacity and the cost of the system often occurs when finalizing the FMS layout. Eventually the finalized FMS layout and configuration is established. The process to

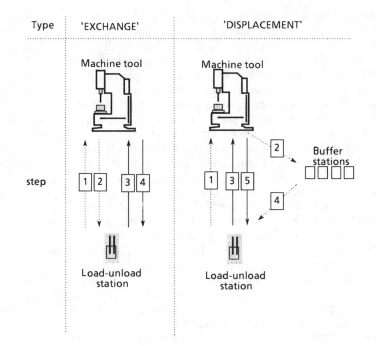

Figure 5.3 Material flow strategies

establish the final FMS layout is very important. It is this layout for which the FMS host system organizes the preparation activities and the internal material flow of pieceparts. The material flow, as organized by the host, is critical as only one of many material flow strategies can be used on an FMS. It is this strategy which will affect the final utilization of the machine tools.

Two extremes of material flow are illustrated in Figure 5.3. The simplest strategy is that of 'piecepart exchange'. With this method a piecepart is set up at a load/unload station and then transferred to a machine. When the work is completed it goes back to the same load/unload station. The material flow is very simple and easy to control, but if other work could go on the load/unload station it must wait until the original piecepart has been machined and returned to the station for unloading. If it does not wait it may block the original piecepart from returning to the station. A more complex solution is to 'displace' the machined piecepart to a buffer store so that a second piecepart can be loaded and sent to a machine. The displacement strategy becomes even more necessary, as the mix of machines, stations, pieceparts and operations increases, to ensure a free flow of pieceparts in the FMS layout.

If a free flow is unavoidable the best compromise can be studied using computer simulation techniques. The objectives of simulation are to imitate, using data techniques, the real world of an FMS. A computer model of the FMS is parameterized on the simulation computer. The FMS may be an existing system, or one that is still in the planning phase. The model is allowed to run, for a specified period, in order to be able to make qualified statements about the FMS's performance. The simulation model enables the operator to experiment with different layouts or piecepart/job mixes running on a given FMS layout.

Simulation computers vary in their design for application. They can either be of the continuous or discrete simulation type. It is more common to find the event-driven deterministic simulation computer used in FMS simulation, although statistical simulation may also be applied (Figure 5.4). A deterministic model measures the performance of an FMS by following the events that may happen for a given period. Each event may cause one of several future events. Priority rules, as to be found in a real FMS, usually limit the alternative effects of an event to one or two actions. With these priorities built into the simulation a very realistic simulation of an FMS is possible. To achieve this the FMS's layouts, process times, alternative actions, etc., must be input into the model. The simulation will only be as accurate as this input data.

Other factors affecting the limitations of computer simulation include costs, computer processing time available and how well the structure of the FMS being simulated is known.

Results that can be achieved with a simulation include:

- comparative analysis of the FMS layout/configuration
- in-depth evaluation of a particularly successful layout/configuration
- optimization of the system, e.g.
    - machine quantities
    - transport system speeds
    - tool store size
- analysis of a production order mix
- evaluation of several optimized processed order mixes
- tool planning analysis.

If the FMS, under simulation, actually exists, then the calculated data can be validated against the real world. If the data are positively validated more faith can be put in any other variations to be simulated.

There are several types of simulation programs or routines available to an FMS user, e.g.

- Simula
- Slam
- GPSS-Fortran

There are also systems on the market whereby an FMS's characteristics need only be parameterized into the computer to create the model, e.g .

- Grafsim
- Model Master

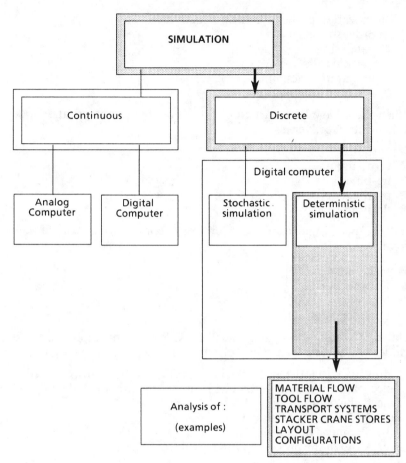

Figure 5.4 Simulation computers for FMS

To execute a simulation the following three main steps are required:

1. Layout of the FMS structure.
   - transport principles
   - machine types
   - piecepart/machine allocation principles
   - ● disturbance strategies
   - routings, etc.
2. Detailing various flow concepts.
   - dimensions of transport system
   - buffer store characteristics
   - machine tool magazine layouts
   - transport unit requirements: pallets, stillages, etc.

3. Optimization of the organization activities.
   - order sequence
   - batch sizes
   - machine allocation
   - preparation activities
   - machine tool magazine loading, etc.

When these have been carried out it is possible to analyse the model in terms of its effectiveness:

- part mix
- throughputs
- up-time
- productivity
- flexibility, etc.

and the performance of the equipment (corner-stones) of the chosen layout:

- machines
- transport
- buffers
- transport units, etc.

Different production strategies will provide different results for the same model layout. The three major criteria which will affect the results are:

1. How to select the next machine to load when transportation of a piecepart is required in the FMS – under the provision that a machine meets the requirements, of:
   (a) NC program available
   (b) Tooling available
   (c) Valid in the process routing for the piecepart.
2. How to empty a machine.
3. How to select the next transport unit for transportation.

The selection of the next machine to load may be based upon:

- any empty machine
- a machine with an empty input station
- a machine with the smallest in-process buffer levels
- the next machine that will become idle by finishing its work-load first.

Machine clearing may be based upon rules such as:

- fetch the transport unit as soon as it has been reported as ready for clearing from a machine
- fetch the transport unit only when the station in which it is positioned is required by another transport unit.

A transport order is an order from the host that the transport system should carry out, for example 'take A, from B, to C'. Selection of the next transport order can be based upon:

- a special priority
- oldest transport order first (FIFO)
- station nearest to transport device receives the next transport order
- chaining of several transport orders together.

The major objective in an FMS design task is to ensure that the machine tools themselves are the system's bottle-necks. This will ensure maximum machine tool utilization when they are not starved of work by some other bottle-neck in the system. This will achieve maximum system productivity. Simulation is also increasingly being used to support the production order mix planning functions. Simulated planning may result in the best order mix selected for the next period – if the manufacturer has the luxury of an order pool to be able to select the next part types to be manufactured. However, the first, non-foreseen, disturbance in the real world may well invalidate the simulated results upon which the FMS's preparation activities have been based (tooling, NC programs, etc.).

5.6 FMS project development steps

When the decision to build an FMS is taken, one of the contracts placed is with the FMS host supplier. This can be directly from the FMS user, for example when the FMS user is acting as the general contractor, or indirectly through the machine tool builder who is employed as the general contractor by the FMS user.

Regardless of how the contracts are placed, the 13 major steps to develop an FMS host are basically the same. Each company has a major role to play in each of the steps. The initial steps involve mainly the machine tool supplier and the FMS user:

1. Planning and design
2. Feasibility study
3. Final layout
4. Contract placements.

Eventually the FMS host supplier plays a major role due to the manufacturing strategies that the FMS host software must provide for the FMS users.

5. Function design specification
6. Project schedule (critical path analysis)
7. Fine function specifications and interface descriptions.

When the first seven steps are completed, through the companies cooperating together, the companies can individually prepare their solutions to the system prior to any joint testing of software, hardware, etc. This involves the following steps for the host supplier:

8. Software creation
9. Generation of the system and parameterization
10. In-house testing of software.

When any new software is ready it has to be tested on the machine tool builder's site before being tested at the FMS site. The commissioning of the system includes the following:

11. Commissioning
12. Acceptance and hand-over
13. Production.

As FMS host technology progresses, not all these project steps are necessary. Some companies provide host functionalities which are truly standard. In such cases the FMS functionality already exists as proven software. It does not need development. Thus steps 5, 7 and 8 may not be necessary. Experience has shown, however, that nearly all FMSs require some fine-tuning, however small. Any special software that is required imposes steps 1–13 on most projects. The order of magnitude for steps 5, 7 and 8 would be correspondingly smaller, however.

How to implement your FMS

Implementation of an FMS involves several stages of documentation (Figure 6.1). These range from the FMS contract to the FMS acceptance protocol.

6.1 Contracts

To develop an FMS, through the joint efforts of various suppliers of different equipment, there are several methods of setting up the exchange of contracts to ensure that every participating company can best safeguard its own interests while also being able to provide the best service to its customers. For instance, the contractual arrangements can be either arranged as a consortium or general contractor type. A consortium can be either 'open' or 'closed' (silent) in nature. With an open consortium the various companies temporarily form a group. The FMS user, i.e. the customer of the group, has a contract with this group. All the companies within the group are known to the FMS user. However, with a closed consortium, the FMS user will not know any or some of the firms in the group. This second case does not really occur very often where FMS supply is concerned because the FMS user company usually wishes to know every firm with whom it is dealing.

If a consortium is arranged, one firm in the consortium may decide to carry out the organizational responsibilities for the group. This company may elect to be the only contact, in the name of the consortium, with the FMS user. This company would almost play the role of a general contractor. The difference is that the technological and financial risks would be spread within the consortium.

Much more common in the field of FMS supply is the general contractor approach. Usually the machine tool builder accepts this role as part of his FMS scope of supply. In terms of cost to the FMS user the supply of the capital equipment, especially the machine tools, is around 75% of the total FMS project costs. Therefore this company carries the biggest financial risk. It is in the general contractor's interest that the project will work and therefore no financial penalties are applied. This interest acts as a guarantee to the FMS user that what he has purchased will work. To achieve this the general contractor must coordinate all the activities of all the supplier companies and the activities of the FMS user

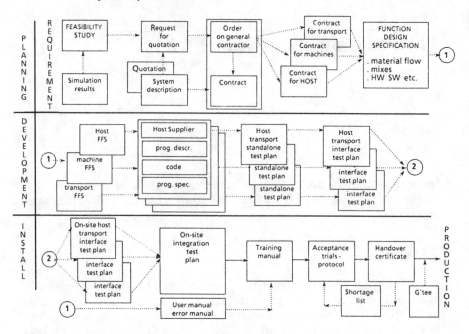

Figure 6.1 The documentated stages to implement an FMS

as well. The exchange of contractual terms and conditions can be either formal or informal. When they are formal the conditions imposed on the general contractor are passed on, on a one-to-one basis, to the supplier companies of the general contractor. With an informal basis the conditions may be passed on differently to the sub-supplier companies.

For systems that are very large and/or contain more than one major machine tool supplier, the FMS user usually acts as the general contractor. No machine tool builder is willing to accept the total risks for an FMS which may include supplies of machine tools from a competitor. The FMS user may either purchase the experience of a consultant, to organize the activities of the project, or may already have the necessary expertise in-house. In all cases a very strong project management is needed, from all parties, especially the general contractor, to ensure the success of the project.

A contract should, in principle, contain the information shown in Table 6.1. A function design specification (FDS) is a very important requirement which should be referred to in the contracts. It should be mutually agreed after exchange of contracts and is the final, valid, legally binding description of the system and the functions of the equipment. It defines exactly *what* is to be supplied by the various supplier companies. It describes *how* the FMS is to be applied in the FMS user's factory. This document is referred to in the contract so that it forms a binding part of the contract. If such a clause appears in all parties' contracts there will be

Table 6.1 An overview of the contents of an FMS contract

General description of the FMS (system description)
General description of the functions of the equipment
Reference to the function design specification
Hardware and standard software scope of supply
Conditions for commissioning
Conditions for acceptance
Price
Commercial conditions
Time schedule
Service and maintenance conditions

no contradiction as to exactly what part of the FMS each party has to supply, however the contracts are implemented. The FDS may be supplied after the contracts are signed; for instance when an FMS has been ordered against a general system description but further technical study is required to finalize the technical scope of supply. In this case the FDS may contradict only the technical contents in the contract – the general system description. This is unavoidable when the document is intentionally written and agreed after the signing of contracts.

When the supply of an FMS is completely standard the FDS and the general system description are almost identical. However, the FDS is required to be personalized to the FMS user. The FMS user company will be named in the FDS, the exact system layout and configuration will be described and the total system hardware and software, with all the functions to be delivered, will be specified.

The FDS is a technical document. It separates the political and commercial contents of the contract from the FDS. The technical supply may change, in content, from the general system description, as the system is designed in the next stages of the project.

An FDS is often ordered simply to see if FMS technology is suitable for a particular production environment, prior to any vast amount of capital being committed. An FMS is not always the most suitable method to manufacture. The experience of FMS supplier companies is often crucial to determine if this is so.

The FDS also serves to protect the suppliers to a known, given, scope of supply. It is not unknown for FMS users to request 'desirable' functions under the pretext that the specified solution will not work without the function.

6.2 Project management

The best FMS project results are obtained when all the parties concerned work within a project-related organization (Figure 6.2).

The FMS host supplier company should work with:

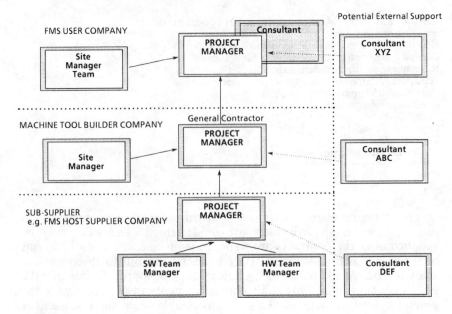

Figure 6.2 An example of a general contractor project organization for an FMS

- a project manager
- a software team leader(s)
- a software team(s), etc.

The general contractor should provide:

- the total project manager
- a site manager
- the level (2 PLC, PC, etc.) programmers if required, etc.

The FMS user should provide:

- a project manager
- a site manager
- the operating personnel, etc.

The host system supplier's software team should test their own programs and work with all the other project personnel. This ensures the most effective method of commissioning the host and controller software. The FMS user, general contractor and the host supplier are involved in steps 4 to 12 of Figure 6.3. Steps 1, 2 and 13 chiefly concern the FMS user and to an extent the general contractor. The major activities for the host supplier company are steps 5 to 12.

From experience, the breakdown of effort for these activities for a major, non-standard, FMS is:

1. Project management   15%

	ACTIVITY	FMS USER	FMS SUPPLIER	FMS HOST SUPPLIER
1	PLANNING AND DEVELOPMENT	X		
2	GENERAL SYSTEM DESCRIPTION	X		
3	BID REQUESTS, DISCUSSIONS	X	X	X
4	OFFER, NEGOTIATIONS		X	X
5	ORDERS			
6	FUNCTION DESIGN SPECIFICATION	X	X	X
7	FINE FUNCTION SPECIFICATIONS		X	X
8	PROGRAMMING		X	X
9	GENERATION / PARAMETERIZATION			X
10	COMMISSIONING	X	X	X
11	TRAINING	X	X	X
12	ACCEPTANCE	X	X	X
13	OPERATION	X		

Figure 6.3 The 13 steps to commission an FMS host

2. Software engineering 15–50%
3. Commissioning   35–70%

Without project management the software engineering and commissioning tasks would probably be 45 percent each of the total project effort. The amount of software engineering and commissioning effort is dependent upon whether the software required to develop the FMS already exists in a tried and tested condition, as standard software, or whether the majority of the software is specific to the particular FMS and must be developed from new. For the host suppliers, who have developed standard FMS software systems, the quantity of machine tools, for instance, is parameterizable and does not require programming into the host. In this way the software engineering costs can be greatly reduced by configuring the FMS with parameterizable software. Such standard software is usually found for the functions which occur across a wide range of FMSs. They are therefore not unique to a particular system and the costs of the creation of this type of software can be spread over many different installations. A parameterizable host may not cover all the requirements for a particular FMS in question. Some unique application-specific software may always be needed. The FMS user should consider that there is a break-even point between the costs of an FMS with standard functions only, not fulfilling every requirement of the FMS user, and a system consisting of only application-specific software which fulfils every wish of the FMS user, which can be very expensive. Software which can be used on many FMS sites and can have its costs distributed over those sites can therefore be supplied at a lower cost to the FMS user. This is the opposite to early FMS sites, where site-specific software accounted for nearly all the software on that site. The entire costs of providing the software had to be covered by the one site. FMS software is maturing to the stage that if the requirements for the FMS remain within the scope of a parameterizable FMS host software suite the costs of that host will be lower and easier to calculate.

Unique and standard software solutions require testing and commissioning effort. To minimize this work a systematic planned approach to the execution of the project is vital. The plan for all activities should be based upon the principles of critical path analysis (or the same system based on probabilities for activity durations, known as a programme evaluation and review technique analysis – PERT). All the companies building the FMS should agree to the completion of their agreed sequence of dependent activities by certain dates. The general contractor, or consortium representative, has the ultimate responsibility to see that this plan is maintained. A further support to a successful implementation is the agreement on relevant documentation required for the project. For example, activities to interface two independent controllers should be carried out to an agreed written specification (a function fine specification) and to an agreed timetable.

6.3 FMS primary and secondary equipment development

Interface specifications should be developed and agreed between the parties whose equipment is to be integrated for the integration of the primary and secondary equipment in the FMS. All machine tools, tool setting machines, etc., should be delivered on-site in a functioning stand-alone condition. Thus only the integration software and the host interface functions are additionally required to integrate the equipment into the FMS. These interfaces should be specified as part of the machine supplier's scope of supply in his contract to the FMS user. If they have been agreed with the host supplier the FMS user can then be assured that his system of machines will be integratable into the FMS. The integration of the host to the production equipment is one of the major activities in building an FMS.

6.4 FMS host system development

The four FMS planning phases include the major activity to developing the system (part of the planning phase):

1. Awareness
2. Planning and development
3. Installation
4. Operation.

Planning and development and installation relate to steps 4 to 12 in the overall project development schedule of Figure 6.3. They are subdivided into further stages through which the development of an FMS host must pass.

6.4.1 Planning

The planning stage consists of the creation of the two important specification documents. These are:

● general system description
● function design specification.

These documents are written by the host supplier and made available to the FMS user and the general contractor. They describe what the FMS and host are to do. All subsequent documents explain how the FMS, or host, are to carry out what they have to do.

(a) General system description
The general system description sets out the aims and the production requirements from the FMS. It establishes the type of machines or processing centres to be used, describes the pieceparts to be manufactured and generally provides an overall framework for the design of the FMS. The original, and often very general, document is written by the FMS user, i.e. the purchaser of the FMS, and is used in their 'request for bids' correspondence. This is taken by the host supplier and developed nearer to the actual scope of supply document which will eventually emerge from this development stage. The general system description is referred to as the basis for the FMS host scope of supply in the contract(s) and order(s) for the FMS. It is necessarily brief as the final solutions to develop the FMS cannot yet be established. A major part of this document is the section referring to the requirements, from the FMS user, of the FMS host.

(b) Function design specification(FDS)
There may be two FDSs to describe an FMS. The first is the document that the general contractor (machine tool builder) will supply to the FMS user. It describes the entire FMS supply. A section of this will cover the requirements of the FMS host, or it may refer to a separate FDS which describes the FMS host. This second FDS is written by the FMS host supplier.
    The host's function design specification is a major document against which the host system can be measured for acceptance from the host supplier's customer. It describes precisely

- what functions are to be achieved by the host
- which interfaces are to be used or developed to run on the host.

The contract will refer to this document as the final binding description of the host scope of supply. In cases of contradiction it will take precedent over the general system description. The hardware's 'scope of supply' is finalized in the function design specification. This determines the configuration of the host computer, its peripheral equipment, input/output ports and the communication procedures and protocols upon which the software functions will run. The function design specification is signed by the FMS user, general contractor and the host system supplier. The objective of this document is to eliminate all ambiguities in each company's understanding of what the constituent parts of the FMS should be (i.e. the capital equipment and the host), and the amount of hardware and software functions that should be supplied for the role they are to play in the FMS.

Specifically, the FDS defines:

- FMS mixes
- FMS material flow
- Software functions
- Hardware supply.

FMS mixes. The piecepart mixes are defined in this document. These mixes are used as the base for testing and accepting the FMS. These mixes are not the limit of the host's administrative capability which should be able to administer other, and probably larger, mixes during the life of the FMS. It is usual that, when the function design specification is written, the future mix of pieceparts for the FMS is not known. Therefore a given mix must be defined in this technical document, which is binding, due to its being referred to in the contract, for all parties to be in agreement about the level of performance with which the FMS host can be accepted.

For the same reasons process mixes (routings) are defined as well as the piecepart mixes. A sophisticated host computer software will enable the definition of the above mixes to be flexible within given boundaries for future expansion of the system. However, the known limit of the host's capabilities will usually be specified. Thus a maximum, minimum and average parameter boundary is always defined.

FMS material flow. The FMS material flow establishes all the possible transfer stations that will occur in the FMS for the specified process routing mix. It may include such piecepart transfer stations as

- raw material store input/output stations
- pallet load/unload stations
- transport system(s)
- machine/transport system stations
- pallet stores
- buffer stores.

The transportation equipment, such as plattens, trays, pallets or still-ages, are defined for the transport systems which will have to carry them.

Software functions. The FDS must describe every standard function, and any FMS site-specific software functions, that the host is to execute. These will include the technical interfaces to the level 2 programmable logic controllers or CNC equipment and to any level 4 or 5 computers, e.g. master host computers, material requirement planning or computer-aided design computers. Every individual function, which each controller at each level is to carry out, is clearly allocated to that controller. The controllers mentioned here include:

Level 4/5	Factory computer	CAD, MRP, area controller
Level 3	FMS computer	FMS host
Level 2	Process controllers	PLC, CNC

The function design specification finalizes all the functions of the host system. Modifications or revisions required of the host's performance, subsequent to this definition stage, can only be implemented if the additional functions are mutually agreed between all the parties who had previously signed the document. Such necessary alterations to the document can occur due to new functions being desired from the FMS user. Alternatively, the host system supplier may require an unforeseen change in order to provide a different solution for a particular function to work. Any such amendments are considered as either mandatory or non-mandatory. The change might be considered as mandatory when the solution, to be supplied, as defined in an FDS agreed previously, would mean the system supplied to the FMS user would not work. No company wants to supply, or have supplied, a system that does not work. Thus agreement to alter the FDS is quite often quickly arrived at. This is also true if a missing function would require the FMS user to carry out so much extra work for the FMS to function that the solution is as good as unworkable.

A non-mandatory change might arise due to an extra function being requested from the FMS user which would only make the supply of the FMS host a more elegant solution. An elegant solution is not always an absolutely necessary requirement. The supply of an FMS host must be cost-effective to the host supplier or they will not remain in such a business for very long. It will, in the long run, depend upon the costs, benefits and delays to the companies concerned, whether they return to the commercial and contractual stages (the FMS development phase) and to agree if any financial recompensations are necessary or not.

6.4.2 Development

The development stage consists of five important steps. These are in chronological order of execution:

1. Hardware development
2. Software development

3. Software implementation and creation
4. Software integration and tests
5. Software acceptance.

These are all carried out at the host supplier's site prior to further tests at the FMS site. It is more effective and less costly to prove as much FMS software as is possible away from the FMS site. Most software errors occur during the software development stage. These errors can be solved more quickly at the location where the software is created than at a remote FMS site.

(a) Hardware development

FMS host software requires the hardware performance of mini-computers or the more powerful of the personal computer range. The size and configuration of the FMS will determine which type of hardware is most suitable for that particular installation. The host must have the capability for multiprocessing and, often, multi-user capability. This can be achieved with standard operating systems available on the market. Whether personal computer or minicomputer, the ability to communicate using real-time dialogues with the machine tools is best achieved with distributed hardware boards using standard communication protocols (preferably programmed into EPROMs). Processing capacity and capability may be required to be extended for certain personal computers through the addition of a co-processing board. In principle, the hardware to achieve the development of an FMS is available on the market. No specific hardware development is necessary. Site-specific configuration of the hardware, in relation to the type and size of the FMS for which it is to be used, needs to be carried out. Figure 6.4 illustrates the decentralized hardware concept that is ideal for FMS. The Unix operating system will increasingly play a more major role in the control of FMS host software.

Sophisticated hardware systems, particularly minicomputer systems, are capable of being parameterized for different hardware configurations and layouts. A particular FMS may require three VDUs, two printers and interfaces to five machine tools. This may dictate a main memory requirement of 4 Mb and a peripheral memory size of 70 Mb. The necessary configuration should be installed at the host supplier's site for testing prior to shipment to the FMS site. The standard operating system, with all the required library and auxiliary programs, are loaded, started and tested. When this has been successfully carried out the standard FMS software can be loaded and tested. A standard system may then be shipped with the FMS software almost immediately after the successful conclusion of the hardware tests. An FMS host, requiring a lot of site-specific software, will be needed at the host supplier's site to assist in the development of this special software. When the hardware is eventually installed at the FMS site the software can be commissioned with the FMS user and general contractor. It is then offered for acceptance and, if successful, accepted and handed over to the customer. The software acceptance may occur separately from any hardware

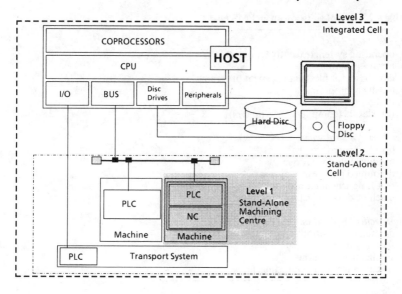

Figure 6.4 Decentralized, configurable hardware concept for an FMS

acceptance. When the commissioning times for software are expected to last over 6 months, as in very large or complex FMSs it is recommendable to have the hardware tested, accepted and handed over to the FMS user as soon as possible. Each individual contract will vary on this point. On a long-running software commissioning contract the hardware will be used to a greater degree even than when it is running purely for its intended function, i.e. to run the FMS. Data transfers are greater and programs with test traces are longer and more demanding on the hardware during the commissioning period. Error situations are forced for test purposes. Extreme production conditions are run and tested. For these reasons the hardware must be continually serviced and maintained even more than during its normal life. When the hardware is accepted and handed over to the customer the guarantees and maintenance contracts can commence so that the hardware is in fact serviced during this demanding period. During on-site commissioning the FMS host supplier should have an identical hardware configuration at his own site. He can then carry out software development, tests and debugging in parallel to any FMS site commissioning, to save time and develop software more effectively.

(b) Software development
A complete suite of FMS software will normally consist of standard software, standard FMS software and site-specific application software. These were shown in Figure 2.3. It will depend upon the type of contract drawn up between the companies as to which types of software are to be

Table 6.2 Types of software on an FMS host

Standard software
- operating system (executive program)
- library programs
- data base- (or file-) management programs
- auxiliary programs
- utility programs
- translators (compilers, interpreters)

Standard FMS software
- operator interface programs
- machine interface programs
- decoupled planning programs
- real-time scheduler programs
- machine data collection programs

Site-specific 'application' software
- manual workstations
- special stores
- specific material flows
- special-purpose machine interfaces

supplied and how. A 'turn-key' contract to a general contractor or FMS user ensures that the FMS supplier supplies only loadable object code and machine code to his customer. This type of supply is in comparison to the supply source code, which a general contractor or FMS user could modify. Object and machine code can only be run by the algorithm for which it is supplied. Thus a specific, and unalterable, function is supplied. The system should be guaranteed to work for the particular FMS defined in the function design specification. It is most likely that the total software supply will contain site-specific software. Very few FMSs can have their function requirements fulfilled entirely by an FMS host supplier's generic standard FMS software.

The FMS host supplier may also supply a machine tool builder, who himself wishes to be the FMS host supplier, with standard hardware and standard FMS software. This software supply may be on an original equipment manufacturer (OEM) basis. Again only object code is delivered but no site-specific software is delivered. This would be delivered by the machine tool builder for his own individual customers.

It would not make good business sense for a host supplier to supply his source code to any other company. All his knowledge and the added value to his hardware supply would then be passed on to his customer, who would eventually end up as his competition.

Table 6.2 lists the types of software that is used in an FMS host.

Fine function specification (FFS). Software development consists of clarifying the functions, as defined in the function design specification, to an even greater detail. It also consists of the creation of the software itself. These details for software creation are described in fine function specifications. The function design specification describes *what* functions are to be performed by the host in a particular FMS. The fine function specification describes *how* these functions are to be carried out by the operators or machine and controllers in the FMS. This specification task is required for functions not already part of the scope of supply of a standard FMS software suite. A fine function specification can be one of two types of document. The first type describes the interface between the host and a human operator (a general process description). The second type, an interface description, specifies the interface between the host and a level 2 controller (e.g. a CNC) or a level 4 or 5 computer (e.g. a CAD or MRP computer). These descriptive documents are used as the specifications for other computer or controller programmers to write their corresponding interface programs. Accurate documents will support error-free exchange of telegrams across an interface. General process descriptions are also used where the functions, after further analysis, are seen to require an even more detailed explanation of how a certain function should work.

The FFS specifies, for a machine or process equipment, the following criteria:

- a machine's mechanical description
- the control hardware and software
- functions (i.e. process of the machine and its relationship between the host and machine)
- material flow within the machine and between the machine and transport system (piecepart transfer)
- machine operation (normal mode)
- machine operation (special modes) – errors, reactions, scrap, re-work, off-line, DNC, exceptions
- interface description between host and the machine.

The interface description is very important. It should include:

1. Procedure
2. Protocol
3. Telegram specifications:
   (a) Title
   (b) Description of structure (header, user information format, trailer)
   (c) Cause (what action lead to the telegram occurring and what was the previous telegram)
   (d) Effect: what response (reaction) should happen now the telegram has been received
   (e) Sequence (within a particular telegram dialogue)
   (f) Alarms
   (g) Program which sends the telegram (host or PLC) – for information only
   (h) Program that receives the telegram (host or PLC) – for information only.

4. Responsibilities (for 1–3):
    (a) Interface (who programs which function)
    (b) Equipment (hardware – electrical, cabling, controller, machine –
         to be provided)
    (c) Software (tests, dates).

The responsibilities (4) are only included in such a document should they
not have been specified in the order, contract or FDS. Each FFS is
developed with the companies concerned (general contractor, FMS user)
until all parties can agree to it. Sub-supplier company agreement is
organized by the general contractor. Several editions may be written to
reach this stage. Only after such documents are agreed can the first steps
to create interface software be commenced. In the case where an FMS
host supplier has his own standard solution the documents are already
available. The above process to develop such a document is only needed
if another equipment supplier cannot agree to provide software to match
this proprietary standard solution.

(c) Software implementation and creation
When software has not already been created (i.e. part of an FMS
standard software suite), or when FMS standard software must be
modified, the tasks to implement new software must be started. It is best
to write FMS software based on a particular FFS with an experienced
programmer. They will be required to write:

1. Program description
2. Program specification
3. Code.

The result is application-specific software (ASW), which might well
subsequently be used as standard FMS software (by the host supplier) on
another FMS site.

Program description. The program description is a brief description of
what a particular program is intended to do and the problem which is
solved as a result of the program. It is written as an aid for other
programmers, who may have to modify the software at a later date.

Program specification. The program specification is a much more
detailed description of how the program carries out the function as
described briefly in the program description. The program, properly
structured, may contain several other sub-programs.
   The program specification should contain:

● program description
● program function specification
● error handling
● installation on hardware
● interface to other host programs (software and dialogues)
● operation of the program

- input data (given files, files referred to, physical storage medium for files, file structure)
- output data (as input data plus an error print-out specification)
- processing (throughput) procedures of the program to solve the problem steps are described, decisions, results, actions, pseudo-code listing
- appendices – detailed layouts, print-outs
- program flow chart
- program listing.

These documents enable the programmer, and other programmers, to maintain or update the program in the future. They are usually only for the internal use of the host system supplier.

Any human interfaces should be detailed for the FMS operators or machine controllers to operate the program. The operation by the FMS user will also be detailed later in a user manual.

These steps up to the coding of a program are interactive. There is feedback from the coding stage, which may possibly affect the program description and specification, until the final working version is achieved. This feedback may reach back to the FFS and even FDS, requiring changes to be made to these documents, but in a properly managed and designed system this should never happen.

Code. Coding of the programs can follow the bottom-up or top-down creation principles or a mixture of both. Programs should be structured with the capability to be configurable and parameterizable. Text strings should not be programmed into the code but be called up from text files. This facilitates the translation of one operator interface language to another language. This minimizes the costs to an FMS user should they require a specific language. High-level languages (Fortran, Cobol, C, Pascal) can be used for non-time-specific functions. The host computer organizes the FMS requiring large data transfers. Cobol, an old and well-proven language, is suitable for these tasks. For time-critical tasks an Assembler language is used.

(d) Software integration and tests
The ASW and FMS standard software programs which are to run on the host must be integrated on to the hardware. This is accomplished with the generation of a parameterizable operating system. All programs require access to the main memory to run. If they cannot all be accommodated in the main memory they will need to be initially stored on peripheral discs. If this is so, how they are swapped in and out of the main and peripheral memories, and into which common areas, pages, segments, etc., is part of the software configuration design task.

The sequence of host program testing is:

1. Individual program test. Each program is compiled and the algorithm is proven to run on its own with test data. Syntax, syntactical and logical errors are eliminated from the algorithm.

2. Host program integration test. Each individual program is integrated into the software system so that it can run with other FMS host software to which it interfaces. System errors are eliminated. Simulation programs are used to assist the host, processing centre or transport system software tests.

Note that during this period, programs which are to run on the PLC's hardware, at the other end of the interface, should be written. When they have reached a level of testing, so that they can run as successfully as possible and independently, they can then be tested with the relevant host program. The PLC/NC software should also be tested with simulation programs prior to connection to the host.

3. Host/machine-controller interface test. The PLC hardware and software are brought to the host supplier's site for testing with the host. This is the ideal situation but cannot always be carried out.

4. Host/machine-controller/machine test. If a suitable host system is available at the machine tool supplier's site the interface can be tested between the host and PLC with the actual, or similar, machine connected to the PLC. This ensures that more realistic tests can be carried out in order to find the maximum quantity of errors possible, and eliminate them, before further tests are carried out at the FMS user's site.

(e) Software acceptance
There should be an internal acceptance of software by the host system supplier company. On acceptance, the programm(s) are released for further testing on the machine tool builder's and/or FMS user's site. The programs should be at the stage where all errors have been cleared, as is practicably possible prior to going on to the next major stage in the building of an FMS – that of installation.

Chapter 7

How to install your FMS

Installation of an FMS involves the testing and commissioning of many computer-to-computer, and computer-to-operator interfaces. These tests must be executed in the correct sequence, starting from the very simplest tests and slowly building up to the unavoidable more complex tests. When the interfaces and functions in the FMS are tested, the operators can then be trained prior to system hand-over. Figure 7.1 provides a general overview, in the form of a critical path analysis (CPA), of the major tasks to install an FMS.

7.1 Communication interface characteristics

An FMS includes many types of hardware which all have some control function or other. Whether a controller is a PLC on a machine, an NC unit or the host computer itself, they all have similar characteristics. These characteristics are:

1. Operator interfaces
   - VDUs, terminals, printers, etc.
2. Communication interfaces
   - machine or processing centre controllers to the host (or vice versa)
   - bus or serial
3. Process control interfaces
   - for level 2 work centres – the actual process/machine being controlled
   - bus, serial or parallel (digital or analogue inputs/outputs, etc.).

An FMS host computer organizes the production equipment and workstation operators in the FMS to a given plan. It does not directly control any process in real time. Thus characteristic 3 does not apply to the host. The host has multiple interfaces of types 1 and 2. Generally the work centres have only one interface of each type (see Figure 4.3).

7.1.1 Computer/controller interfaces

Within each controller there are different types of software functions. These functions are:

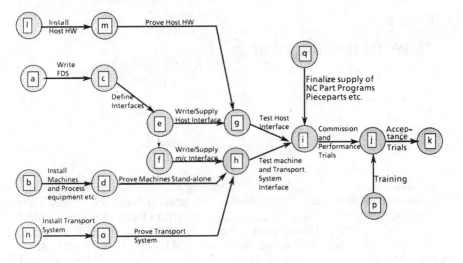

Figure 7.1 A CPA showing the major tasks to install an FMS

1. Standard system operating software
2. Standard FMS
3. Application specific FMS software
4. Interface handler/driver software
5. Process software.

A controller may have several of each type of software function (except for the operating system). The host will definitely have several of each type (again except the operating system, unless a co-processor board is used). For example, the host will have such a program as the 'machine control' program within its software suite. This program, or set of programs, administers the production equipment (e.g. the work centres) in the FMS. These programs organize and monitor the status of the work centres by communicating with the PLCs of level 2. This is achieved by sending or receiving telegrams. These are transmitted following an agreed hardware procedure. The format of the telegrams have also to follow an agreed software protocol. The function fine specifications determine how each controller should react to a specific telegram, i.e. to the user information contained in the telegram. The telegram's cause is also established in this specification.

Once the installation of the host hardware is completed the host's FMS software can be loaded and tested. As mentioned in Chapter 5, the machine's software should have been tested at the system supplier's site and/or at the machine tool builder's site. The advantage of the latter is that the software can be tested with the machine hardware integrated with the machine controller software. Thus the tests will be more realistic. The final tests commence on the FMS user's site. It is practicable to eradicate all software bugs prior to going on-site. Whilst the tests are being carried out on the FMS user's site, a back-up team at the host system supplier's site can eradicate errors which are found whilst carrying out tests at the FMS user's site, thus saving time.

7.1.2 Interface test characteristics

The steps listed in Table 7.1 are required to establish a communication interface to a particular coupled program in the host. The host's machine-control program is used as an example.

Each activity is aimed at proving the software functions correctly, and, if not, isolating the sources of errors at each stage to assist the elimination of problems. A specific sequence of activities ensures that any software bugs can originate from only one source. These major activities are summarized in Table 7.2.

The tests, up to the controller's single tests, are primarily to prove the functioning of the level 2 software. As this is done a certain amount of test-result feedback also supports the testing of certain host software, but chiefly the major host tests commence from the host/controller integration tests. In a machining FMS the level 2 controller test activities consist of various DNC tests. The host/controller integration tests consist of various activities involving FMS tests (Table 7.3).

Table 7.1 FMS software commissioning sequence

Step		Activity		
1.		Functional design specification		
2.	(a)	Function fine specifications		
	(b)	Software creation		
		Controller-specific		*Host*
3.	(a)	Stand-alone test	(b)	Host single test
	(c)	Support test (simulated host)	(d)	Host integration test (simulated PLCs)
4.	(a)	Cabling – physical		
		– logical		
5.		Format		
6.		Controller functions		
7.		Controller single tests		
	(a)	– DNC 1–3		
	(b)	– Transport system		
	(c)	– DNC 4–6		
8.		Host/controller integration test		
		– FMS 1–5		
9.		FMS integration test		
10.		Training		
11.		Acceptance		

Table 7.2 Test sequence to isolate software errors

1. Determine the functions which the host's control program should carry out *(function fine specification)*.
2. Write program(s) to achieve (1). This includes programs on the host computer and in the (level 2) controller *(software creation)*.
3. Test individual host program on its own *(host single test)*. Single tests are used to test a single individual program's functioning. This also applies for the software which is to run in the CNC's PLC *(controller single tests)*.
4. Test programs *(host integration test)* using a simulation program to simulate the machine's hardware and software.
5. If necessary the machine controller software should be tested at the general contractor's site with the host (if a host computer is available). The work-centre hardware, e.g. the machine which the controller is to control, need not be integrated with the controller software at this stage if the interface is known to work already *(support tests)*.
6. Test programs at the FMS user's site with the other work centres which have successfully completed their own controller single tests. At this stage the tests are carried out with host on-line programs. Real-time scheduling is simulated *(host/controller integration tests)*.
7. Test all work centres with all host FMS functions. Real-time scheduling is not simulated *(FMS integration tests)*.

Table 7.3 DNC and FMS test activities

DNC tests
DNC 1 – up- and down-load NC programs.
DNC 2 – as DNC 1 plus tool loading/unloading dialogue for tool-offset dialogue prove-outs.
DNC 3 – as DNC 2 plus pallet load/unload transfers to prove pallet zero-offset dialogue.
DNC 4 – as DNC 3 plus transfer of pallets into machine to prove the piecepart flow at a machine.
DNC 5 – as DNC 4 plus the processing (cutting) of pieceparts.
DNC 6 – as DNC 5 but for two to n machines in a system consisting of n machines (host DNC performance test).

FMS tests
FMS 1 – machines organized under host control (piecepart flow). Process plans written for *complementary* operation of the machines.
FMS 2 – as FMS 1 but for *interchangeable* machine operation only.
FMS 3 – FMS 1 and 2 tests combined (i.e. *hybrid* operation of the FMS).
FMS 4 – as FMS 3 plus the integration of further host on-line functions (piecepart set-up dialogue, synchronization, tool flow, etc.).
FMS 5 – Synchronization of transport system, machines and host, etc. (When possible this test is carried out as early as possible for early rectification capability of the system status when the system has been disturbed due to tests being carried out).

7.1.3 Objects of the tests

The DNC tests are carried out before any FMS tests. This is to ensure that the core functions in an FMS work before any complex FMS function tests are commenced.

DNC. The DNC tests are a specific type of controller single test. The object of the DNC tests is to prove the up- and down-loading of NC part programs, tool data, machine data collection (e.g. alarms/system messages), etc., for the machining centres.

FMS. The FMS tests are a specific type of host/controller integration test. The FMS tests are designed to prove the working of the automatic material and tool flows under the organization of the host computer. Process routings are input into the host piecepart specifically. Following this input the machines should be supplied with work according to these routings. The tests cover the ability of the host to organize the supply of work to the machines with an interchangeable or complementary machine tool allocation of the machines to the piecepart. Factors affecting the supply of work to machines are piecepart types, batch sizes, pallet set-up quantities, operations per set-up, cycle times and the number of production orders live in the system.

7.2 Test sequences

The sequence of the test must be taken in a specific order when testing every level 2 controller in order to isolate any errors that may occur. The sequence, per machine, is listed in more detail under steps 1 to 8 in Table 7.4. The elimination of the possibility of multiple error sources minimizes the effort to find the source of an error. A systematic approach to FMS commissioning reduces costs and time to get the FMS up and running.

7.2.1 Preparations for testing

To carry out any software tests, sufficient master data – to create the FMS data base – and specific equipment must be provided by the FMS user at the correct time. The steps to test an FMS, as shown in Table 7.5, indicate the type of data and equipment that are necessary to execute the tests. For example, DNC tests on machining centres require the following master data:

1. NC programs
2. Tool plans
3. Tool data
4. Transport unit (e.g. pallets) data
5. Pallet offset data, etc.,

Table 7.4 Detailed sequence of integration steps

Step	Test	Description
1.	Stand-alone	The machine's controller software is written, pre-tested without the host, and is seen to function successfully so that the machines operate autonomously.
2.	Physical	Cabling is layed and tested between the host and the controllers at the FMS users.
3.	Logical	Check protocol/procedure handling at the interfaces on the installed cabling.
4.	Format interface	Test the controller's successful reception and sending of previously specified interface telegram formats. The telegrams are sent from the host using a test program (simulation) and not the host machine-control program. Initially the down-loaded telegrams are tested, then the up-loaded telegrams.
5.	Controller functions	The actions and reactions of the controller's software to the telegrams sent from the host are tested. The machine must carry out the correct processes in the right sequence before responding to the host with the correct telegram(s).
6.	Single test (controller)	The host's machine-control program is integrated with the controller via the interface. Correct actions and reactions of the host are tested.
7.	Host/controllers integration	These tests bring in more and more equipment and host functions as each are proved to work successfully. The optimum sequence, after all work centres have completed the controller function tests, is: (a) Tool setting machine (b) DNC 1–3 (c) Automatic transport system (d) DNC 4–6 (e) FMS 1–4 (f) Single tests (non-machining centres) (g) Integration tests (non-machining centres).
8.	FMS integration	These tests prove the performance of the entire FMS modules (work centres/host) after they have achieved test level 7(g) above. Level 2 and 3 controllers run parallel/simultaneously in real-time operation.

with the following equipment:

(i) tools
(ii) machine tool
(iii) tool-setting machine, etc;

FMS tests on a machine tool require additional master data:

1. Process plans
2. Fixture data
3. Production orders, etc.,

with the following equipment:

(i) fixtures
(ii) component set-up stations

Table 7.5 Equipment and data required for the commissioning of an FMS

Test	Machines	Function	Set-up orientation	Operations	Production orders	Pieceparts
DNC 1	n	NC PP transfer				
DNC 2	n	tool exchange				
DNC 3	n	tool setting				
+						
transp	$n + ts$	transfer process				
DNC 4	n	transfer process				
DNC 5	n	metal cutting				
DNC 6	n	parallel performance				
FMS 1	1	interchangeable	1	1	1	10
	2	machines	1	1	1	20
	3		1	1	1	30
FMS 2	n	complementary	1	1	1	30
	n	machines	1	2	1	30
FMS 3	n	hybrid machines	1	2	1	40
FMS 4	n	performance	1	2	1	40
			2	2	1	40
			n	3	1	60
			n	3	2	60
			n	n	2	60
			n	n	20	n
FMS 5	n	synchronization	–	–	–	–

(iii) transport system
(iv) components, etc.

A qualified computer operator and a qualified NC operator are also required for the tests. They should be authorized to make any necessary hardware and/or software changes.

7.2.2 Points to consider during commissioning

(a) Approach to integration (concept)
The approach to commissioning an FMS can be carried out, following the procedures listed above, in two different ways. The approach can be either:

1. To test a single module type, e.g. all the machining centres, from the simplest stand-alone test to the most complicated FMS-5 test before

moving on to the next module, e.g. a wash machine, and bring this up to the FMS-5 test level. Thereafter the entire mix of modules is integrated with the host computer into the final FMS configuration, one at a time, or

2. To test every module type (the machining centres and wash machine) up to a specific test level (DNC I) together before proceeding to the next test level (DNC 2). In this way the whole FMS is brought up to FMS-5 level together before continuing the integration of the entire FMS layout.

The first alternative is preferable as, with the machining centres tested first, a core module of the FMS is brought into a production mode before adding further, non-productive modules, and increasing their automation levels. This has advantages for all parties concerned. The system during non-test periods and the machine-tool builder (if it is not the general contractor) has fulfilled its contractual obligations earlier. For this benefit to be taken advantage of, the parties concerned not the general contractor) has fulfilled their contractual obligations earlier. For this benefit to be taken advantage of the parties concerned must agree that all tests take priority. Otherwise the host supplier company will be put at a disadvantage if it cannot get the machine tools back, to continue host commissioning, because the FMS user company wishes to continue production on its new machines.

(b) Work-centre access

Leading on from the two alternative approaches to commission the FMS is the consideration for the supplier company's access to the FMS site and equipment. The ideal situation in which to commission an FMS is where the FMS user's systems development department organizes the installation of the FMS for the FMS user. This department should control the site until official hand-over to the FMS user. Thereafter this systems development department can hand the system over to the FMS user's production department. Often, owing to the pressures to manufacture pieceparts, the production department wishes to have access to the work centres which have already been proved to work in a stand-alone mode. There is no reason why this should not happen as work centres are expensive items of capital equipment and should be utilized as much as possible. The FMS user/system supplier's access to the work centres must be clearly agreed, prior to starting the commissioning stage, to avoid delays and hinderances to testing, which are costly. Commissioning should always take priority to achieve the shortest duration for installation.

(c) Applied test effort

FMS user companies often believe that a supplier company will carry out the commissioning tests faster if more people are applied to the tasks. This is not so for the FMS host supplier company. When testing the interface software (for functions which could not be adequately proved using the host and the machine simulation programs away from the FMS site) it is best to have the computer and controller programmers on-site to test their own interface software. These engineers can only work certain hours effectively (ten hours a day up to a maximum of two shifts daily for a short intense period). It is of no use applying more engineers to the task to shorten the test period unless they are deeply involved and motivated in the development of the particular interface and control programs; programmers are only human. Other commissioning engineers might take over other tests on a third shift. To use the third (night) shift is only practicable if such alternative tests are carefully planned, so that they do not disturb the main interface tests. This is not always possible as the computer/controller may need new software generations or configurations for each test. It is a time-consuming task to regenerate an FMS host. If regeneration is not required, the third shift can be given over to the FMS user for production purposes, with the machines in stand-alone mode. The secret of a short commissioning period is good software, good software commissioning engineers and excellent planning.

(d) Organization
Pre-planning is essential to achieve effective commissioning. The FMS user has to prepare components for material-flow tests. Master data (the data base) must be created and input into the computer. Test equipment, such as data-line monitors, must be available. Relevant personnel should be on-site at the correct time, and be aware of the tasks they have to carry out. As a result of the planning every participant/company must be aware of the responsibilities, actions and timings of the tasks which they have to carry out. The use of the CPA supports this approach.

7.3 Training

The creation of the controller's and host computer's application software, along with the testing of the communication interfaces, should be carried out by highly qualified software and system engineers. The knowledge of how to run a system, designed around complex software and hardware, must be transferred to the FMS user's qualified production personnel. Training should start long before the system is tested. The FMS user begins to understand the system from the very first feasibility study. The detailed training of the FMS user company's personnel covers the handling of the controller's and computer software and the system's equipment. The FMS user's system engineers receive an understanding of the FMS whilst jointly developing the system's functional design specification and the function fine specifications.

Subsequent to this know-how transfer, the operators are trained at the stages shown in Table 7.6. The chronological sequence of the different types of training are shown in Figure 7.2.

From the very first FMS development stage (contract/FDS/FFSs, etc.) the FMS user's personnel gain knowledge about the FMS and its

Table 7.6 The major training phases

1. Software development at the system-supplier's site on development software. The feedback from the operators assists further software development and system acceptance.

2. Software commissioning familiarization training whilst the commissioning tests are being carried out at the FMS user's site. Whilst working with system engineers, and 'looking over shoulders', handling of the system can greatly be left to the FMS user's personnel. Short informal training periods after specific functions have been successfully tested assist the transfer of knowledge.

3. Provision of an official training period directly before the system is offered for acceptance to the FMS user. The aim is to ensure that the system can be operated by the FMS user's personnel during the acceptance trials. This assists system acceptance.

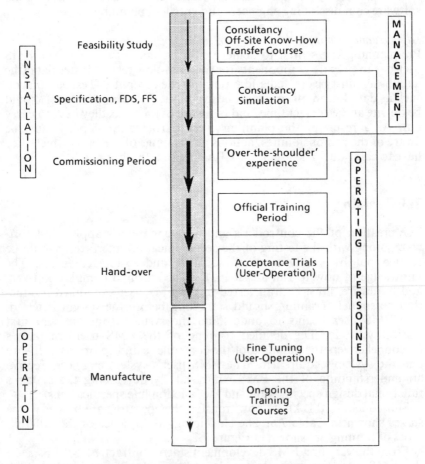

Figure 7.2 Stages of training during the development of an FMS

functions. Specific official training is required to fully transfer the host-operating know-how to the correct people. During commissioning, familiarization training (over-the-shoulder and short unofficial training periods) is carried out. Prior to acceptance a formal planned training period is required to enable the FMS user's personnel to run the FMS unaided during the acceptance trials. This assists acceptance as the FMS user will feel adequately trained to use the FMS after the general contractor and host system supplier companies are no longer on-site.

Training covers handling the hardware, operator interfaces (such as screen dialogues, listings, etc.) and recovery situations. A detailed user manual should explain how to load the FMS's capacity with work, prepare the FMS to carry out the work, react to the host's output (as the host monitors the FMS on-line) and how to recover the system when operations fail (using the error reports). The programmers, who carry out the training, should also assist in writing the user manual in cooperation with the FMS user's operators, to produce a document which is meaningful to the operators. The transfer of know-how is further increased using this method.

When a standard parameterizable system is to be installed the training can be straightforward. It can be carried out during system commission at the host-supplier's site as all the functions have been previously developed along with their training requirements.

A training schedule is required which should define:

aims
functions for personnel to be trained for
sequence
duration
personnel required
equipment required
dates/times.

Training can be likened to learning how to drive a car. The operator needs to know how to drive the FMS but it is up to him where he drives it to, i.e. which pieceparts to produce on the FMS.

7.4 System acceptance

When all parts of the FMS are successfully tested, the system is handed over to the FMS user company for local operators to run. Every function, described in the function design specification, is demonstrated and offered for acceptance. As they are proved to work the functions are individually accepted by the FMS user's representative, who is authorized to sign off the system. Further demonstration of accepted functions is not usually required. When all functions are accepted (as listed in the officially agreed acceptance trial function list), the system itself is accepted and officially handed over to the customer. Should all functions not work correctly a previously agreed level of accepted functions will allow the FMS user to sign-off the system with the provision that the erroneous functions will be corrected straight away. A benchmark as to whether to accept the FMS or not is generally when the FMS can produce pieceparts, unhindered by the erroneous functions in the host. Hand-over usually determines the change in property rights. The FMS becomes the property of the FMS user, who subsequently puts the system to good use.

7.4.1 Host acceptance

The host acceptance activities involve:

- acceptance trials
- hand-over
- production.

These activities must be correctly planned.

(a) Acceptance trials
A host acceptance trial function list (ATFL) describes every FMS host function, as defined in the FDS, which is to be offered for acceptance by the host supplier. The general contractor and/or machine tool builder will have their own ATFL for the complete FMS. The host functions are demonstrated using real, not test, data. If the function being demonstrated is seen to work it is accepted by the FMS user and need not be demonstrated again. The ATFL is often in the form of a tick list. As each function is accepted it can be 'signed-off'. Notes may be made against the function's acceptance when improvements are agreed to be installed or if a minor sub-function fails. Any corrective actions are agreed to be cleared (i.e. to clear the error and re-offer the sub-function for acceptance) within an agreed time schedule.

In this way a previously agreed level of accepted functions will enable the FMS user, or the general contractor, to accept the FMS host from its supplier even though minor functions may be outstanding.

(b) Hand-over
When acceptance is granted, the complete FMS, or just the FMS host, can be handed over to the FMS user even though not all functions are accepted. This usually occurs when sufficient functions work to provide effective production of pieceparts. It is agreed, prior to hand-over, that the functions which did not work will be corrected and offered for acceptance as soon as possible.

It is at this stage that the host's hardware and software:

1. Guarantees, warranties
2. Service and maintenance contracts
3. Short-list repair activities

can commence. Property rights are exchanged at this stage.

(c) Production

When the FMS (host and machines) has been handed over it can be put to work by the FMS user to manufacture pieceparts.

7.4.2 Total FMS acceptance

It is usual for the machine tool builder to accept the host from the host supplier. The acceptance for the total FMS equipment (host and machines) is given by the FMS user to the machine tool builder or general contractor.

7.5 Post-acceptance activities

When the system has been handed over to the FMS user several FMS host activities can commence:

1. Service and maintenance contract for the computer hardware and standard software. This is usually covered by a separate contract. Optionally this may have been agreed to start as soon as the hardware was accepted.
2. Application and standard FMS software guarantee. Usually, for one year, the host system supplier agrees to solve software bugs that occur, free of charge, if they are the fault of the system supplier.
3. Post-acceptance improvements. Functions that could not be accepted as they were erroneous are improved, tested, offered for acceptance and handed over if accepted.

It may be one or two years on very large FMSs before every non-critical bug is captured and solved. Very occasional occurrences of physical situations may give rise to the type of bug which would have been impossible to foresee at the software development stage. These situations are very rare indeed.

It should also be remembered that a highly automated, and therefore productive, system, running continually over three shifts per day, requires more servicing than a system running over one or two shifts per day.

When the system performs to everybody's satisfaction the system is often demonstrated by FMS user, general contractors and suppliers alike as a reference system. To achieve this level of system performance, and acceptance, it is in the interests of all parties concerned to cooperate together and to commission the FMS as quickly and cost-effectively as possible.

Chapter 8

How to apply your FMS investment for profit

A company deciding to install an FMS will be looking at plans that will have long-term far-reaching effects that quite often are not realized at first. It could lead to a total change in a company's thinking and structure. Successful installation of an FMS may show up current bad working practices and concentrate the corporate mind into improving present processes in the company.

There are many potential benefits that accompany the introduction of FMS technology. However, there may also be technical and commercial risks to be analysed and understood prior to embarking upon an FMS strategy. Once understood, they can be minimized or eliminated. Installation of an FMS must be carried out right first time. The impact of an FMS is immediate to the processes which are included in the FMS environment. An FMS also has effects on other departments to which it is integrated. The particular FMS strategy employed will be company-wide and must be supported, and committed to, by the entire management at all levels. This beneficial knock-on effect can only be realized when the company's manufacturing strategy is analysed as a whole. The benefits of the chosen FMS strategy will be felt over several departments in a company.

8.1 Types of FMS investment

There are several reasons why a company will invest in the new FMS technology. These can be summarized as:

- a pilot investment
- a showroom investment
- a rationalization investment.

For over 20 years most FMS investments have been of the first type – a pilot investment. 'Leading-edge' companies have invested in FMS to learn about the technology. This has been seen as giving them an advantage over their competitors. Other companies invest in a pilot scheme to catch up with these leading-edge companies. The introduction of an FMS enables the technology to be evaluated and the benefits diffused throughout the corporation. The company also learns how to install the technology. This is often seen as one of the most effective

Table 8.1 The major reasons for rationalization investment

1. Replacement of plant
2. Expansion of plant
3. Strategic (e.g. research and development)
4. Removal of existing bottle-necks
5. More efficient/effective use of existing plant

means of bringing CIM into a company, especially when an FMS is self-financing, as an FMS is in fact a small CIM factory on its own.

Today, smaller companies are looking to the benefits from FMS. They cannot rely on the outcome of pilot sites and are more dependent upon the FMS suppliers who have gained their experience from the installation of pilot, and other FMS, sites. Their requirement is for the supply of standardized, proven FMS software.

Showroom investment is mostly applied by FMS machine tool suppliers to indicate to potential customers that they have the technology which they are selling. FMS host suppliers also demonstrate their capabilities on host demonstration systems. In-house FMSs are built not only for demonstration but also to actually manufacture pieceparts for the machine tool builder's own equipment. Recently, with the introduction of working FMSs, companies are installing FMSs more and more for their own rationalization reasons. The company perceives that it can reduce unit production costs for its pieceparts, thereby increasing profits, sales and competitiveness.

The major reasons for rationalization investment are listed in Table 8.1. These are the most common reasons to install FMS.

8.2 Analysis of all the benefits

Application of an FMS necessitates the integration of departments, levels of automation, information and processes. This integration gives rise to various benefits for the company through the process of synergy when the whole company looks at the potential of FMS. Even if such an analysis undertaken proves FMS not to be applicable, such a study usually finds other problems in the company's current methods. Should FMS technology be applicable, the benefits and the risks must still be understood for the best rationalization investment to be made. To achieve this an investment appraisal should be carried out. For this to be a successful appraisal the current costs of production must be compared with the future ones of an FMS. Most accounting systems do not provide an accurate view of the causes of current costs with, usually, lump sums hidden in the general overheads of a department. It is crucial to know where current costs are arising to make a fair comparison of present and future systems.

It is of benefit if the company's accountants understand the technology of FMS to understand its advantages. This will reduce the risks of error in any evaluation of an investment appraisal. To oversimplify a point: it is not enough to justify such an investment as an FMS on only labour cost savings, either direct or indirect. Many companies regularly use the direct labour cost savings benefit per unit method only. This may be applicable for small items of capital equipment purchase but it is not relevant for a manufacturing system which will encompass the activities of one or several production departments.

It is not uncommon for only 8 percent of a piecepart's production costs to be attributable to labour. Material can account for 50 percent of production costs and overheads for 42 percent of these costs. An FMS does not always reduce labour requirements and never to the much hyped levels of zero-manning. Manning levels are reduced but a different level of labour skill is required. More intelligent, responsible, highly trained operators are needed, which may give rise to higher costs per operator. It is not reasonable to compare the costs of a current and future system on the basis of such a small element of a production facility's costs. It is more reasonable to compare the higher efficiency of capital investment, and the obtainable flexibilities and productivities in the potential future system with the alternatives of the current production system. When the FMS is to replace the production of pieceparts from only a part of an existing production facility the comparison can be quite difficult. Costs may be incurred in the residual existing system due to the removal of part of its total piecepart mix.

The cost accounting methods should be able to analyse the tangible and intangible elements to be able to quantify any investment benefits. All aspects of an investment must be considered. This will include the total investment costs, which can then be compared with the operating costs and savings.

8.3 Types of investment appraisal

An overview of current standard appraisal methods indicates the pros and cons of these techniques, as used in industry today, for the application of FMS appraisals.

There are various types of investment appraisal. Not all of them are suitable to appraise an FMS investment. The alternative methods are found in Table 8.2.

The payback method is simple, and suitable only for a comparison of various alternatives as a first assessment. It measures the ratio of net profit to costs to establish the number of years required to recoup the investment. An arbitrary company figure is set, e.g. three years until payback, to establish the validity of a project. However, an FMS may be in use for 10 to 15 years before the machine tools need replacing. This method does not measure the profitability after the payback period; it only looks at the liquidity implications. Thus only projects with rapid

Table 8.2 Investment appraisal methods

1. Payback method (PB)
2. Return on investment (ROI)
3. Net present value (NPV)
4. Internal rate of return (IRR)
5. NPV adjusted for capital utilization
6. MAPI method

Table 8.3 Evaluation of net present value

$$NPV = SUM_{t=1}^{T} \frac{(\text{net cash flow})_t}{(1+r)^t}$$

r = interest rate on long-term cash
t = year of project
T = economic life of project in years

capital return seem acceptable. A very large FMS requires one to two years before full optimal production can be achieved. A small FMS requires 6 months to a full year. During this period little or no cost savings will be realized. By the FMS user fine-tuning an FMS from his own experience, after the hand-over of the system from the supplier companies, the actual profit and returns can be increased over the ensuing years of operation by a level which cannot be foreseen or estimated at the initial appraisal stage.

The ROI method is slightly better but is also only suitable for an initial appraisal. This method measures the ratio of net profit in a 'normal' year to the total capital outlay as a percentage. An FMS is designed to be able to manufacture a random mix of pieceparts which may change from week to week and will certainly change from one year to the next. It would be hard to establish what a normal year's net profit would be.

A better approach is the NPV method, which looks at cost flows, their timings and discounts and therefore their values over the economic life of an FMS project (see Table 8.3). If the NPV is equal to, or greater than, zero, then the target rate of return is greater than the interest on the borrowed investment, and the project is therefore deemed acceptable.

The IRR method is the same approach as the NPV method. However, it measures the IRR when the NPV is set to zero. Thus the profitability of the project is measured. An improved version of the NPV method is achieved when the NPV is adjusted for capital utilization. Net profits and any residual value from the FMS are discounted at the present-day value. For this value the costs, also in terms of NPV, are deducted. The resulting NPV is amortized over the project's life to obtain the average annual NPV. This average NPV is measured as a ratio of the average amount of capital tied up, thereby giving a measure of profitability of the project as charged at the discount rate fixed by the company.

The MAPI method (as developed by the Machinery and Allied Products Institute in the 1950s) is similar to the capital utilization adjusted NPV method, but it also compares the present equipment's usage costs with the investment of the FMS. The method is suitable for replacement or new capital equipment projects but it assumes that the advantages of the new equipment are fully known from day one. Again, an FMS can be fine-tuned by the operators, who will proceed along a learning curve as they use the FMS. The full capacities and capabilities of an FMS can only be learned at a later date.

Whichever investment appraisal method is used, all costs and savings (or, if measured annually, expenditures and incomes) must be identified. For a full appraisal of outflows and inflows the benefits of tax allowances for capital equipment purchases, capital equipment depreciation allowances and investment grants should also be included in the analysis.

8.3.1 Total investment costs

The total investment costs will include the expenditures arising from:

1. The FMS supplier(s)
2. Consultancy
3 Use of software houses
4. In-house costs.

As the first three types of cost arise based on a quoted price, and a subsequent contractual arrangement, the amounts of monies to be spent are fixed to a high degree of certainty. Only if the scope of supply is changed by the FMS user after the contract has been agreed is it likely that further unforeseen costs will arise. It is the in-house costs which are usually underestimated, if estimated at all, and which can invalidate the results of an investment appraisal. An investigation for an FMS investment may bring to light benefits to the company which have nothing really to do with the intended FMS and its cost savings. The study may show up inefficiencies which would have remained hidden in the company's production methods had the study not been undertaken. Some of the in-house savings may occur as a result of actual cost savings which could be realized without any FMS investment. An analysis required for an FMS investment might show savings to be made by the company just by ceasing to carry out an activity.

(a) FMS supplier(s)
The FMS user can place the contracts either directly with a general contractor, usually the machine tool supplier, with a consortium of supplier companies, or divide the contracts between the supplier companies, in which case the FMS user company takes on the role of general contractor itself. If an FMS requires only one type of machine tool, and therefore machine tool supplier, it is advisable to place a single contract

on to the machine tool builder. The supplier agrees to provide an FMS with a given performance for a given piecepart mix. This simplifies the arrangement for the FMS user. When an FMS requires several types of machine tool a single contract approach is often not possible. A single machine tool builder is not always amenable to take on the responsibilities of the supply and performance of another machine tool builder's equipment. They may even be competitors. Thus the type of FMS to be installed affects the ways an FMS can be organized contractually.

The machine tool hardware, and its commissioning in an FMS, can cost up to 80 percent of the total FMS costs. The computer hardware and software supplies the other 20 percent of the costs. The machine tool prices will not be higher for an FMS than for their supply as stand-alone machine capability. Some additional costs will arise from their upgrading, from their stand-alone capability, to that of a machine tool that can be fully integrated into an FMS, i.e. the interface driver and functional software. The other major costs arise from the required peripheral equipment such as transport system (piecepart and tooling), tool setting stations, buffer stations, pallet load/unload stations, pallets and fixtures.

A realistic cost analysis must show whether the additional investment in an FMS host not only supports/justifies the additional FMS hardware and software expenditure, through increased productivity, but also maintains the cost benefits for the life of the FMS's installation. The productivity comparison can also be made not only between a group of machine tools, with or without the addition of an FMS host, but also between an FMS and the current production system(s)' cost/productivity characteristics.

(b) Consultancy
Consultancy can be obtained from:

● independent consultants
● the machine tool builder
● the FMS host supplier.

Independent consultants charge for their services but have the advantage of being neutral in any advice as to which FMS supplier is suitable for a particular FMS solution. They provide useful support during the appraisal and general requirement phase of an FMS project's life. They do not have, however, the detailed knowledge of any particular FMS supplier's solution. For this the FMS user must rely on their relationship with the FMS supplier. During the planning, installation and operation phases of an FMS the FMS user receives a great deal of consultancy from the FMS and FMS host suppliers apparently free of charge. The know-how of these suppliers is, of course, part of the contract prices.

(c) Use of software houses
A company with very large resources may wish to provide its own FMS solution. For this, the service of an external or internal software house

might be employed. A great deal of responsibility will then remain with the FMS user, who will have, or have to obtain, the knowledge required to successfully install an FMS. Most software houses can provide effective competent software but require the instruction as to the fundamentals of an FMS, from FMS experts, to even begin to be able to supply the right software solution.

Alternatively, software houses might be employed to supply a sub-system solution for part of an FMS (e.g. a piecepart store) for which existing software, or software adapted from a well-proven standard, can be applied.

(d) In-house costs
In-house investment costs occur during the planning, development, installation and run-up phases of an FMS project. The costs will arise from:

1. Preparation of plant:
   (a) Widening doors
   (b) Preparing floors:
       ● levelling
       ● AGV tracks
       ● drainage
   (c) Providing power and services
   (d) Raising ceilings.
2. Provision of:
   (a) NC part-programs
   (b) Tooling
   (c) Fixturing
   (d) Robotic grippers.
3. Training of personnel.
4. Adjusting CAP facilities.

There may also be some 'costs' which are in fact beneficial to the company whether the FMS is purchased or not:

● adapting the piecepart design (rationalization) to FMS requirements (e.g. for fixturing)
● piecepart mix rationalization
● revenue from sale of machines to be replaced
● elimination of bad working practices.

8.3.2 Operating savings

The potential for an FMS to bring tangible accountable benefits to a company can be summarized under the following cost reductions:

1. Labour
2. Working capital assets
3. Materials.

Other intangible benefits arise from:

4. Personnel development
5. Flexibility
6. Overheads.

(a) Labour
Savings are possible from both direct and indirect labour reductions. These savings will not only arise in the new FMS but will also concern other departments with which the FMS is to be integrated.

(b) Working capital assets
Savings are possible in terms of reduced work-in-progress and inventories. The inventories for raw material, intermediate goods and finished goods can be reduced when shorter lead times and quicker throughput is achieved with FMS. Lead time for a piecepart is the sum of net processing times plus waiting times for a piecepart. Waiting time for a piecepart arises from the piecepart either having to sit in a buffer or be transported to a machine or load/unload station. The relationship of waiting time to net processing time can be in the ratio of thousands to one for a non-automated workshop. With the automation of material flow through FMS technology this ratio can be reduced to a factor of tens to one. FMS technology creates shorter lead times, which enables reductions in work-in-progress. No value is being added to a piecepart while it is standing around. A machine cutting metal earns money. An idle machine costs money.

(c) Materials
The direct costs of materials, i.e. costs per unit, can be reduced for unprocessed, semi-processed and sub-assembly materials. With increased quality the yield of material usage rises. This reduces the need, and therefore costs, of re-work or scrap replacement. Scrap replacement costs involve the cost of the lost piecepart and the replacement piecepart. Re-work costs involve the overheads of the repair. There is also an intangible cost saving to be achieved here – that of a decrease in late deliveries arising from occurrences of scrap or re-work. Batch quantities can be reduced if replacement pieceparts for scrap or re-work need not be taken into account when planning production levels.

(d) Personnel development
What may initially look like a cost is in fact a long-term saving. The training of the indiginous work-force to work with the newer and higher levels of technology reduces the dependence on external know-how. An improvement in working conditions through automation will have beneficial results as well.

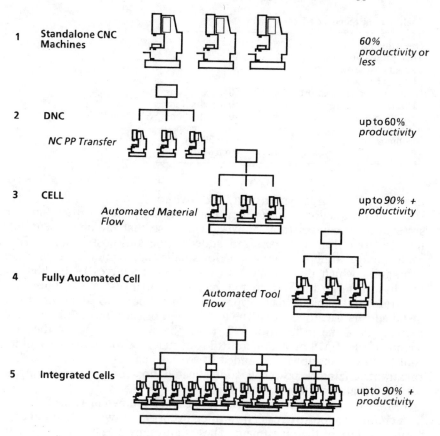

Figure 8.1 A stepwise approach to the expansion of an FMS

(e) Flexibility
Flexibility to the changing market demands or random events occurring in a production system enable a more efficient utilization of capacity (see Chapter 4).

(f) Overheads
With increased capacity utilization subcontracted work can be brought in-house, thereby providing cost savings. A more realistic allocation of overheads to all pieceparts produced by the company will enable better costing and control.

8.4 Self-financing the FMS

Providing that a surplus cash flow is realistic for a particular FMS investment, there is no reason why the installation cannot be self-

Table 8.4 The economic effects of FMS

Operating profits	112–310%
Total production costs	14–27%
Labour cost savings	30% +
Material cost savings	13–15%
Inventory and work-in-progress	50% reductions
Floor space	50% reductions
Lead times	40% reductions
Machine utilization	30% increases
Machines required	from 30 to 6
	from 80 to 12

financing. Very large systems may take two to three years to be brought into full production. However, a company may start with a smaller system and expand it in a stepwise fashion so that the investment can finance itself from the increased added value and cost benefits. This evolutionary strategy is preferable for smaller companies, or even large companies which do not have vast financial resources to be able to purchase a large FMS from the very start of investment. Figure 8.1 illustrates this expansionary approach. When one FMS island has been installed it is true to say that the duplication of such an island does not require the same installation effort for the second island as the first island. If one FMS host can control four machine tools, a 16-machine-tool FMS can be slowly expanded to over a number of years by either re-parameterizing a powerful sophisticated host or by duplicating a series of smaller simpler host solutions.

FMS investments have given rise to the results shown in Table 8.4.

A cumulative positive cash flow often occurs after two and a half years from the start of the investment. These figures are specific to particular FMS projects but they show that financial advantages are possible. The FMS acts as a catalyst to achieve such benefits in manufacturing industry.

Chapter 9

Four examples of FMS

Four European examples of FMS are described to illustrate different manufacturing strategies that can be included under the scope of FMS. Two are from the United Kingdom and two from the Federal Republic of (West) Germany. These two countries have invested heavily in FMS technology. All four systems have been developed over the past four years and are modern examples of successful FMS installations.

9.1 The HNH (Hattersley Newman Hender) FMS

An FMS host computer has been developed for a machining system installed to manufacture high- and low-pressure bodies and caps for water, gas and oil valves. Figure 9.1 illustrates the system layout.

This flexible manufacturing system, installed at Hattersley Newman Hender Ltd., Ormskirk, UK, has been designed for the manufacture of 2750 different types of pieceparts. It has been developed for a high throughput rate for pieceparts with short machining cycle times.

The FMS consists of primary and secondary facilities. The primary facilities include five universal machining centres and two special processing centres. The secondary facilities consist of auxiliary facilities such as tool setting and manual workstations.

9.1.1 The system layout and facilities

(a) Machining centres
Two 5-axis horizontal 'out-facing' machines and five 4-axis horizontal machining centres work under host control in the FMS.

All the machines have a rotating pallet changer, each with two pallet buffer stations. These stations transfer pallets to and from the transport system (eight automated guided vehicles) and also to and from the machining zone in the machine tools. The five universal machining centres have two magazines, each with 40 tool pockets per magazine. Thus each machine has a capacity for 80 single pocket tools. The two special-purpose out-facing machines (OFM) each have one magazine of 40 tools. The magazines are either loaded in an interactive mode by the operator in dialogue with the host computer or manually with the aid of

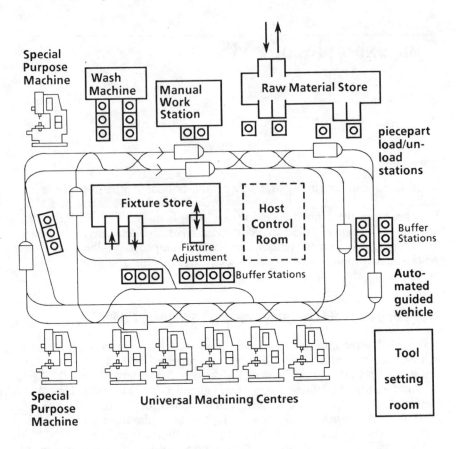

Figure 9.1 The Hattersley Newman Hender FMS

a data-acquisition control terminal, which is linked with the machine's numerical controller.

(b) Processing centres
The system incorporates two types of processing centres – a wash machine and two manual workstations:

Wash machine. Two conveyor belts (one for input and one for output of pallets) can each convey three pallets. The wash booth can accommodate up to seven pallets. The pallets are washed in the booth and turned upside-down to allow them to drip most of the water out of the pieceparts before being rinsed and dried with blown air.

Manual workstations (ring-fitting area). The system's two manual workstations enable operators to fit metal sealing rings manually into the valve bodies. The host computer supplies the operators with working instructions via two data-acquisition control terminals. The operators fit the rings into each valve body (which are supplied by the transport system to the workstation). When the job has been completed, the operator informs the host computer through a dialogue using the terminal. The host computer is responsible for organizing the removal of the piecepart from the workstation.

9.1.2 HNH secondary facilities

The FMS consists of auxiliary stations and facilities.

(a) Auxiliary stations
Load/unload stations. The FMS has four piecepart load/unload stations. The host works in an interactive mode with the operators. The host computer ensures that the operators are supplied with the information and instructions concerning which pieceparts are to be loaded and/or unloaded. Loading and unloading is performed with the instructions being displayed on a further four data-acquisition control terminals, one at each station. The host computer organizes the delivery and removal of empty and loaded pallets at the stations.

Fixture-setting station. In order to readjust the fixture on a pallet into a different setting to carry an alternative piecepart type, the host computer can communicate interactively with an operator, at the fixture store, through a seventh data-acquisition control terminal. The purpose of this operation is to enable the fixture concerned to be used for another product type mix.

Administration of tools. Tools are assembled manually. The dimensional offsets of the tools can be checked on a tool-setting machine. The tool-setting machine generates a bar code in order to identify the tool that has been set. This code is used later during an interactive host and operator dialogue, at the machine tool magazine, for the loading and unloading of tools. Tools are exchanged at the machines manually. The host administers tool lives and the required tool exchanges.

(b) Auxiliary facilities
Transport system. The transport system consists of a controller (microprocessor), and eight automated guided vehicles (AGVs) guided by submerged inductive control wires. An AGV battery charging area is also included in the transport system. The host computer supplies transport orders to the transport system controller which determines which AGVs are needed to carry out the order.

Buffer stores. The FMS has 20 buffer stores in order to store the empty and loaded pallets while they are waiting to be taken to another transfer station (i.e. a load/unload station or a machine tool etc.).

Maintenance area. Empty and loaded pallets are taken into and out of the system at a special transfer station. This facility caters for pallets that may be damaged or need servicing or for scrapped pieceparts.

Raw-material store. Containers with raw material (pieceparts such as forged valve bodies, etc.) are stored in the stacker store which is located in front of the load and unload area. The store is served by two fork-lift-stacker cranes. It supplies the piecepart containers to the load/unload operator via motor roller conveyors. The store can accommodate up to 80 containers.

Fixture store. A second stacker crane store has space for approximately 120 fixtures for their storage when they are not used live in the FMS. At any one time the fixtures are assigned to a specific pallet. They can, however, be reset by an operator when the stacker crane supplies the fixtures, via a motorized roller conveyor, to the manual workstation for the resetting of a fixture. The fixtures are fetched from, and delivered to, the FMS by means of two further input and output motorized roller conveyors. These fixtures are collected by AGVs for transfer into the system.

9.1.3 Production strategy

The strategy for production is fulfilled by the host through the following parameters:

1. Administration of 5000 NC part-programs.
2. Up to 2750 different pieceparts to be machined in the FMS. Each piecepart requires at least one NC part-program. As some of the workpieces need more than one operation (that is, more than one NC part-program), the host computer is required to manage the total of 5000 part-programs.
3. 26 different pieceparts can be manufactured simultaneously in the FMS (a mix production strategy).
4. Piecepart pallets administration. The FMS has 120 identical pallets, each of which can carry one fixture. A total of 64 different fixture designs are available which allow all the 2750 workpieces to be incorporated into the FMS.
5. Tool administration. The FMS requires a total of 600 tools. These are made up of 140 different tool types. The tool type mixes in the magazines are not changed but administered as tool sets. Sister tools are exchanged when a master tool becomes blunt.
6. Ring administration. There are 50 different types of rings to be fitted into the relevant valve bodies in the ring-fitting area. The rings are made of various types of metal.

9.1.4 Production parameters

Production at HNH is determined mainly by the following factors:

1–1000 parts per production order
12–17 production orders per active production mix
two 'filler mixes' per 1–10 production orders
up to 26 piecepart pallets in the system at one time
two to three shifts per day
NC program run-times of 2–40 min (average 5 min)
time spent by workpiece in the FMS (throughput/workpiece) 10–140 min (average 80 min)
typical transport time 2 min
up to eight pallet settings per piecepart (average two settings)
up to seven operations per pallet setting (average five)
● up to five alternative allocations of interchangeable machine tools to one piecepart operation (the five horizontal machining centres).

Three main routes are used which are determined by the different tool-set mixes. Various other routes are also managed by the host computer. The principal routings are:

load – horizontal machining centre – wash – unload
● load – horizontal machining centre – horizontal facing machine – wash – unload
load – horizontal machining centre – wash – ring-fitting area – horizontal facing machine – wash – unload.

The other major production parameters are itemized in Table 9.1.

The host control technology is provided by a Siemens FMS host computer. The host computer organizes the activities that are required for production. These are listed in Table 9.2.

9.2 The Rover LM-500 FMS

A flexible manufacturing system and host at Rover Cars Ltd., Birmingham, UK, has been developed for the manufacture of 16-valve cylinder heads. The object of the host development is to ensure optimum machine capacity utilization, to achieve high product quality and to enable a flexible response to changes in production and market requirements.

The FMS is used for mixed-batch and series production. The FMS host controller coordinates three production areas. The first area is for machining pieceparts, the second is for finishing, including the assembly of pieceparts, and the third is for supplying raw materials, removal of finished parts and the organization of a quarantine buffer.

Interconnection of these three production areas is provided by two fully automatic robot clamping areas which clamp pieceparts, supplied to the FMS on transport containers, on to pallets which then carry the

Table 9.1 An overview of the HNH FMS equipment

Production equipment

5 × FM 100 (KTM) horizontal machining centres:
  2 magazines each with 40 tools,
  pallet changer with I/O and machining station

2 × KTM 4-axis horizontal out-facing machines:
  1 magazine with 40 tools,
  pallet changer with I/O and machining station

1 × wash machine (Duerr):
  3 input, 5 machining, 3 output stations

1 × tool-setting machine (Zoller)

1 × transport system with 8 AGVs (Wagner)

20 × buffer stations along the routes

1 × input/output station for empty/full piecepart pallets

1 × stacker store for 80 raw-material containers (Dexion)

120 × piecepart pallets with mechanical coding

1 × stacker store for 120 piecepart pallets (Dexion)

4 × piecepart load/unload stations

2 × manual workstations

1 × fixture setting station

Material flow system:
● automatic workpiece transport
● manual tool exchange

---

work into the FMS. Under host control the robots also unload the completed work from the pallets for removal of the work from the FMS. Within these three production areas the host computer supplies the processing stations with necessary tooling and part-program information and also provides the inductive transport system with transport orders to supply the machines with pieceparts.

The host's material flow control modules organize material supply in accordance with the pieceparts' process plans. These can be adapted by the operators from one production order to another using the host if it proves necessary to change a production order's process sequence.

Quality control is in the form of random part measurement organized by the host. The host blocks any machine responsible for exceeding tolerances and identifies to the operator the pieceparts which have been in the quarantine store since the last random sample inspection. These quarantined pieceparts are then inspected by the operator.

9.2.1 The system layout and facilities

The layout of the three production areas integrated into the FMS, the raw material, machining and assembly areas is shown in Figure 9.2.

The FMS layout incorporates:

Table 9.2 The HNH FMS host functions

Data base management:
Management of master and control data:
- factory calendar
- planning sheets
- workpiece pallets
- tools
- NC programs
- production orders

Capacity planning of machining centres:
Tool requirements
Pallet requirements
Utilization/loading

Preparation:
Tool
Pallets
DNC

Material flow:
Control of production facilities
Machining centres with DNC
Transfer of NC programs to the machines
Material flow control
Material tracking
Order control
Production facilities check
End-of-work switching
Production data acquisition (PDA):
- order management
Machine data acquisition (MDA):
- mode change
- fault messages
- organizational interruptions
Loading statistics
Automatic synchronization

Monitoring:
Data logging
Message logging
Lower manpower shift
Visualization of the system
Machine loading statistics
Shift log

(a) Raw-material supply area
- autonomous transport system with two trucks
- input and output stations for blanks and production parts (10 manual workstations)
- connection to a transfer line via a robotic cell
- storage/quarantine station for 16-valve cylinder heads and cam-shaft covers (30 stations)

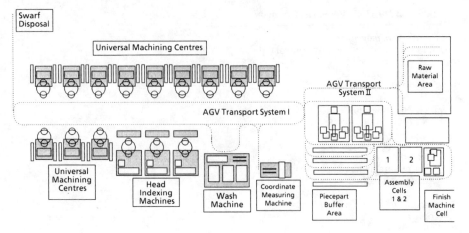

Figure 9.2 The Rover LM-500 FMS

● storage/quarantine station, including an intermediate buffer, for the delivery of the diesel cylinder heads as they are removed from the supply transfer line (70 stations)
one service station for the manual inspection of workpieces and the exchange of transport containers
a total of 100 transport containers each with 8 or 16 piecepart locations.

(b) Machining area

11 machining centres each with 80 magazine pockets, a pallet changer and a station for chip containers
3 head-indexing (bore) machines each with a pallet changer, an additional FIFO input/output piecepart buffer and a chip container
● 1 wash machine with a wash robot so that several pallets can be washed simultaneously
1 CMM measuring machine
● 1 chip collection station
● 1 tool-cutter setting machine
● 3 service stations for manual inspection and scrap/refinishing work
● 1 transport system with 11 automatic guided vehicles (each with 2 transport saddles) and 67 buffer positions for pallets.

(c) Assembly and finishing area

2 robot assembly cells for the assembly of valve seats to valve guides and heads to covers for the 16-valve cylinder heads
1 finishing cell.

Each cell consists of several special-purpose machines and a robot. Total quality control is integrated in the cells.

(d) Robotic clamping cells

The material supply, machining and assembly areas are linked with two fully automatic robotic clamping cells. Each clamping cell consists of:

- 1 conveyor for the transfer of a maximum of 9 pallets
- 10 stations for the raw-material transport containers
- 1 robot and several manual buffer store areas.

In order to minimize transfer times, all stations, except for the machining centres, are designed in such a way that a transport vehicle can deliver and pick a pallet up simultaneously.

9.2.2 The FMS host control

The host organizes the production for a piecepart mix of ten different part types. The pieceparts are produced in an average batch size of 500 parts per batch. The host is fully integrated to the production facilities listed in Table 9.3.

The host organizes manufacturing through the main activities listed in Table 9.4.

9.3 The Vickers FMS

The third example of an FMS has been developed in West Germany. The Vickers flexible manufacturing system was developed at Vickers GmbH, Bad Homburg, West Germany, to produce a range of automobile power-steering servo-pumps. The flexible manufacturing system is designed for the production of small pieceparts in a large number of variants whilst maintaining a high throughput despite short machining cycles. The production plant manufactures a mix of batches simultaneously. The host enables the current production mix to be switched at short notice to a new order mix.

The system supports a just-in-time concept of piecepart ordering. Material and information flow in the FMS enable orders to be processed exactly in accordance with customer requirements. The pieceparts are manufactured to a uniform high quality, and in the quantities required, to a tight schedule.

The FMS layout, shown in Figure 9.3, was developed using computer simulation to resolve the conflicting objectives of high throughput, machine utilization and quality. Despite the large number of machine tools, transport systems, buffer stations, work-holders and a fully automatic robotic loading/unloading area, the host computer enables the system to maintain a very high level of performance. The transport system, in particular, with its complex network of routes, places high demands on the on-line material flow control of the host computer.

The sequence in which the pieceparts are machined is controlled in accordance with process plans as laid down in the master data which is stored in the host. These are generated by the FMS user. The material

Table 9.3 The LM-500 FMS equipment

9 × machining centres
3 × head-changing (bore machines)
2 × assembly cells
1 × finishing machine
2 × automatic robot clamping areas
1 × measuring machine
1 × transport system
1 × input and output system for blanks and finished parts
1 × store for diesel cylinder heads
1 × store for petrol cylinder heads
1 × cutter setting device
1 × service station

Table 9.4 The LM-500 host functions

- Control of the processing machines
- DNC (direct numeric control)
- Release of a machine for processing
- Management of the tools in the machine magazines and of the pieceparts on the pallets in the machines
- Control of the automatic clamping area
- Control of the material supply/removal system
- Control of tool-setting activities
- Capacity planning:
  – machine allocation/loading
  – piecepart pallet planning
  – tool requirement planning
- Random quality measurements – machine-specific
- Material tracking
- Quarantine material control and administration (buffering parts measured between random samples)
- Management of the raw material and finished-parts buffer
- Information gathering:
  – printing data
  – logging messages
  – visualization/plant image
- Management of master data
  – plant status data
  – pallet data
  – fixture data
  – tool data
  – process routings/plans
  – production orders
  – NC programs
  – works calendar
- Management of control data
- Transferral of NC programs from a CAD computer to the host computer

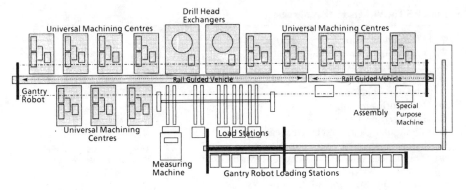

Figure 9.3 The Vickers FMS

flow control program of the host calculates the sequence of machining operations from the process plans and works out an optimum assignment of machine tools for the pieceparts' operations. The transport commands from the host are then sent to the transport system and monitored to ensure that they are correctly executed.

The FMS host's capacity planning module provides the plant operators with a planning tool to enable production orders to be planned accurately. Orders are planned for their batch quantities to specific due dates with the object of optimum use being made of the available resources.

Should there be any breaks in production, e.g. a power failure, the FMS host's synchronization module enables production to be continued automatically, from a particular point in the operation, without excessive machine down-times.

Shifts involving reduced manning levels, e.g. night shifts, are planned with the support of the host computer. The host computer includes an information system which informs the plant operator which tooling and raw materials are required for each machine and order. An operator communication and visualization system, especially designed for this FMS system, reduces the number of personnel required in the control area to a minimum. Only a few operators are needed for the control and monitoring of the entire flexible manufacturing system.

9.3.1 The system layout and facilities

The pieceparts produced are servo-pumps for cars and commercial vehicles. The number of piecepart variants ranges from 40 to 60 different types in various fixture set-ups. The average batch size varies from 100 to 5000 pieceparts per batch. The production strategy is one of mix production.

The production equipment in the system is listed in Table 9.5.

Table 9.5 The Vickers FMS equipment

- 13 machining centres
- 1 special-purpose machining centre
- 2 drill-head indexing machines
- 1 assembly machine
- 1 washing machine
- 1 measuring machine
- 1 tool-setting device
- 16 computer-controlled buffer areas
- 2 transport systems (automatic)
- 2 rail-guided vehicles; 1 gantry robot with a double gripper and various conveyor belts
- 1 automatic load/unload station
- 1 import/export station for piecepart pallets
- 1 tool flow system (manual). The tools are changed manually on the basis of a computer-supported plan
- 1 transport unit tracking system. The transport units are provided with electronic chips each with their own identification codes

9.3.2 The FMS host control

The host computer carries out the organizational activities listed in Table 9.6.

9.4 The KWU FMS

A flexible manufacturing system has been developed at the Kraftwerk Union (KWU) plant in Muelheim, Germany, for the manufacture of turbine blades. The KWU FMS was developed for the processing of medium and very small batches of twisted turbine blades. This has enabled KWU to gain technical and price advantages in their markets. The production plant enables flexible adaptation to variable production methods. These methods are dictated by the non-standard geometrical configurations of the blades. The production strategy conforms to a 'just-in-time' concept whereby the material flow of the FMS permits order processing which is coordinated to the requirements of the subsequent assembly department. Turbine blades are produced which are of the correct quality, in the correct amounts and at the correct time.

The variability in the production engineering requirements necessitated comprehensive control functions from the host. These were implemented on the host computer, and special demands made of the on-line material flow control and the planning functions. The processes for a set of blades, as required for a single turbine, are divided into several production phases. One production batch corresponds to a production order. The order data, production process plans, piecepart data, tool data and NC data (including tool plans) are transmitted to the host computer from a master production computer. The optimum

Table 9.6 The Vickers host functions

1. On-line functions:
   - control of the production equipment
   - machining centres with DNC
   - transfer of NC programs to the machines
   - material flow control
   - material tracking
   - order control
   - resource checking
   - end-of-shift mode change
   - quality control
   - production data acquisition: order management
   - machine data acquisition
   - mode change
   - fault messages
   - organizational disturbances
   - load statistics
   - automatic synchronization

2. Off-line functions:
   - resource planning for production periods
   - machine scheduling
   - transport unit planning
   - tool requirement planning
   - planning for tools resulting in current load/unload lists and setting lists

3. User functions:
   - parameterization of the plant layout using interactive forms
   - password control

4. Enquiry functions:
   - listing of data
   - logging of messages
   - reduced manning shift
   - plant visualization

5. Management functions:
   - management of master and control data
   - works calendar
   - process plans
   - transport units
   - tools
   - NC programs
   - production orders

production sequence is determined by the operator with support from the host during a planning session.

The supply of tools into the manufacturing system, and their removal, is controlled by the host computer. Optical signals are used at the system's input/output stations for identification purposes. An automatic

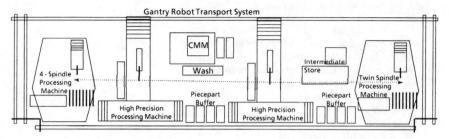

Figure 9.4 The Kraftwerk Union FMS

tool transport system ensures that the appropriate tools, once set, are available in the process machine magazines. Piecepart carriers (pallets) are not used as the blades have to be processed from all sides. Instead a uniform clamping facility was developed for the entire range of blade types. Identification of pieceparts is maintained logically in the host as no machine-readable identification of the piecepart is available.

An operating interface and visualization system, specifically developed for this plant, makes it possible to run the FMS from the control station with a minimum of personnel.

9.4.1 The system layout and facilities

The layout of the system is shown in Figure 9.4. The production periods are planned for a 2- or 3-shift period. The piecepart mix consists of two types of raw material.

The raw material is pre-processed from either milled parts (for solid high-pressure blades) or forged parts (for low-pressure blades). There are

Table 9.7 The KWU FMS equipment

1 control station
1 host computer
4 machining centres
1 wash booth
1 measuring machine
1 tool-setting device
1 parts-marking system
1 transport system comprising two gantry robots
1 input/output store for milled parts
1 input/output store for forged parts
5 piecepart buffer stores
16 tool-pallet link areas
21 tool pallets
1 transport car for fixtures
5 piecepart fixtures

Table 9.8 The KWU host functions

- Automatic transportation of pieceparts (no pallets; no machine-readable identification)
- Control of the input and output of pieceparts, stores management and material tracking
- Automatic transportation of tools (by machine-specific pallets into the machine magazine; no machine-readable tool identification)
- Control of production facilities (transport system, machines, marking system)
- Management of fixtures
- DNC administration (not tool data)
- Control of the tool-setting activities
- Administration of the machine-specific commissioning of tool pallets (utilization planning)
- Machine capacity planning
    - piecepart planning for the allocation of machines (optimum batch sequence)
    - tool requirements planning
    - alternative and emergency strategy planning
- Information functions
    - printing data
    - logging messages
    - visualizing the plant
- Interactive operator dialogues for input/output of data
- Master data management
- Control data management
- Transmission of data to and from the master host to the FMS host
    - order data
    - production work plans
    - piecepart data
    - tool data
    - NC programs including tool plans

approximately ten different piecepart types, processed in an average batch size of 200 parts. Table 9.7 lists the FMS equipment.

9.4.2 The FMS host control

The host controller executes the functions listed in Table 9.8.

Index